Art and Landscape
in Charleston and the Low Country
Spoleto Festival USA 1997

S P A C E M A K E R   P R E S S

Washington, DC
Cambridge, MA

ART AND LANDSCAPE

IN CHARLESTON AND THE LOW COUNTRY

A Project of Spoleto Festival USA

by John Beardsley
with contributions by Roberta Kefalos
and Theodore Rosengarten

Principal photography by Len Jenshel

Art and Landscape
in Charleston and the Low Country
A Project of Spoleto Festival USA

Front cover: *Field Work*
by Martha Schwartz
Title page: *Cypress Swamp Garden*
by Adriaan Geuze
Back cover: *Rice, Rattlesnakes, Rainwater*
by Martha Jackson-Jarvis

Publisher: James G. Trulove
Art Director: Sarah Vance
Designer: Elizabeth Reifeiss

Printer: Palace Press International

Library of Congress Catalog
Card Number: 97-062363
ISBN 1-888931-17-5

Spacemaker Press
602 E Street, N.E.
Washington, D.C. 20002

Contents

Artists

6
Foreword by Nigel Redden

12
Human|Nature
by John Beardsley

30
In the Master's Garden
by Theodore Rosengarten

66
Magdalena Abakanowicz

72
Herb Parker

80
Patrick Dougherty

88
Philip Simmons and Pearl Fryar

94
Martha Jackson-Jarvis

102
Mary Lucier

110
Esther Mahlangu

116
Charles Simonds

124
Thornton Dial

132
Ronald Gonzalez

142
Martha Schwartz

150
Adriaan Geuze

158
Artists' Biographies

166
Acknowledgments
Spoleto USA Board of Directors

Above all things, a festival evokes the spirit of a particular place. Spoleto Festival USA is unthinkable outside of Charleston, and Charleston is a particularly fertile source of inspiration for much of what is special about Spoleto Festival USA. The traditions of Charleston—its streets, churches, and theaters, the sense of life lived at a different pace—have all inspired the festival's programs since the first season in Charleston in 1977. Anyone who has heard a chamber music concert in the Dock Street Theater knows that the space performs along with the extraordinary musicians whom Charles Wadsworth brings to the festival series. The ambience of the Circular Congregational Church lent a unique brilliance to our 1997 production of Benjamin Britten's church parable, *Curlew River*. And who could forget the wonderful dancers of the Balé Folclórico da Bahia holding an impromptu dance for hundreds outside the Sottile Theater on George Street? These performances were only a few of the hundred or so of the 1997 season that together became an exploration in which we invite our audience to participate, taking them to any of five theaters, three or four churches, as well as outdoor venues scattered around the peninsula and out to Middleton Place and Kiawah Island. Piccolo Spoleto invites our audience to another thirty-odd churches, theaters, halls, and rooms. The festival is a musical exploration of Charleston as audiences go from the Dock Street Theater to the Galliard, from Grace Episcopal Church to the Cistern at the College of Charleston, from the Sottile to the Cathedral of St. John and St. Paul.

But to be truly successful, Spoleto Festival U.S.A. is not simply for those who attend performances. At their best, festivals can transform a particular place and a particular time. For seventeen days, the arts become the chief business of Charleston, and the city takes on a new energy, a special vitality. Banners, window displays, spontaneous performances on street corners, dancing in Marion Square, special programs on television and on radio, all attest to something different in the low country at the end of May and the beginning of June.

In 1997, we extended the exploration of Charleston by asking John Beardsley to invite a group of sculptors, landscape artists, and designers to come to Charleston to examine the physical environment in and around the city. The resulting exhibition, called "Human/Nature: Art and Landscape in Charleston and the Low Country," brought twelve artists' projects to downtown Charleston and the area west of the Ashley River, to Berkeley County and Middleton Place. Most of these projects were to be in places that the festival does not normally reach; most were also to be accessible to the public without charge. We hoped that the artists would find the setting of Charleston to be intriguing, and we hoped that they might discover places in and around the city where our audience members, many of whom come from outside South Carolina, might not otherwise visit. We wanted to extend the sense of excitement and occasion that Spoleto Festival U.S.A. brings to Charleston to parts of the city that the festival had not previously touched.

Additionally, we wanted to build on a distinguished legacy of the visual arts at the festival. Both Spoleto Festival U.S.A. and the Festival of Two Worlds in Spoleto, Italy, the American festival's forebear and until recently, its companion festival, have always included the visual arts as well as dance, theater, music, opera, and other performing arts. Some of the exhibitions have been particularly distinguished. In 1962, David Smith created his remarkable *Voltri* series as part of "Sculture nella Città," an exhibition that included the work of some thirty sculptors sited throughout the medieval city of Spoleto. More recently, in 1991, Spoleto Festival U.S.A. mounted "Places with a Past: New Site-Specific Art in Charles-

Foreword by Nigel Redden

ton," a landmark exhibition curated by Mary Jane Jacob, which also brought new work to unexpected spaces within an urban setting. That exhibition was a great success on many levels. Perhaps the most unexpected result was how certain pieces were adopted by different groups and institutions in Charleston. "Places with a Past" built bridges within various communities that would not have existed without the stimulus of a particular artist's vision.

Our organizing principle for "Places with a Past" was the past, perhaps the past of Charleston, perhaps a more generic past, whether remembered or created, an historic past or a personal past. For "Human/Nature," it was the natural environment, whether transformed by human intervention, like the rice fields of Cypress Gardens, or as untouched or untouchable as the sometimes extreme weather of the Carolina coast. We hoped some artists would be inspired by the landscape of Charleston; others might comment on it; and a few might change our perception of places that have become so familiar to those of us who live in the city as to become almost unnoticed.

As I had hoped, artists responded to our invitation with a great generosity of spirit creating works that drew on many elements that make this region unique. Mary Lucier created a dreamscape of historical places, imagined people, and the ominous approach of a storm. Magdalena Abakanowicz gave definition to a grand entrance to the city from the ocean with her stunning *Hand-like Trees*. Patrick Dougherty's whirlwind of maple saplings traced a path that countless feet had worn through Washington Park. Ronald Gonzalez's ghostly figures developed an extraordinary patina during the course of the exhibition, evoking the passing lives of those buried at Magnolia Cemetery. Martha Jackson-Jarvis explored the singular role played by African slaves in the development of rice culture in South Carolina in her beautiful work at St. Luke's Church.

A few of the works will remain in Charleston. Pearl Fryar's and Philip Simmons' delightful garden will grow and change. Charles Simonds' whimsical clay figures in the rediscovered grotto at Ashley Hall School will remain until time and weather have completely eroded them. South African artist Esther Mahlangu's vibrant *Portal to America* will also remain as a temporary reminder of her reaction to visiting America.

This exhibition would have been impossible without the generous support of many individuals who are recognized in the acknowledgments. I do want to give special thanks here to the City of Charleston. The consistent support of city departments and city crews was especially important to the success of "Human/Nature." I also want to thank those in addition to the city who made their facilities available for projects that were definitely outside the scope of what they usually do: the Historic Charleston Foundation, the Gibbes Museum of Art, Middleton Place, Ashley Hall School, Magnolia Cemetery, the Bennett Hofford Company, Cypress Gardens, the Medical University of South Carolina, St. John's Reformed Episcopal Church, and St. Luke's Reformed Episcopal Church. I want especially to thank John Beardsley for his vision of the exhibition and, finally, I want to thank the artists who participated for the energy, enthusiasm, and talent that they gave to their projects.

Nigel Redden, General Director
Spoleto Festival U.S.A.

Overleaf:
McLeod Plantation Allée, James Island

Drayton Hall,
a property of the National Trust
for Historic Preservation, Charleston

Human|Nature

By John Beardsley

This book is the legacy of a special project of the twenty-first season of the Spoleto Festival U.S.A., an exhibition entitled "Human/Nature: Art and Landscape in Charleston and the Low Country." While the festival regularly features a visual arts component, only once before—in 1991—has the organization commissioned a large collection of site-specific art. The 1997 exhibition featured twelve projects by thirteen artists dispersed around the city and the surrounding countryside, offering perceptive glimpses into the low-country environment for Spoleto visitors and native Charlestonians alike. It revealed the landscape to be both a cultural artifact and a dynamic natural system in which humans play a part. "Human/Nature" demonstrated the enormous appeal of the region's native environment, but it also surveyed some of the varied cultural patterns and abundant social history apparent—or disguised—in its landscape. If the exhibition explored familiar terrain, then it did so with the goal of seeing it anew.

While creating a composite picture of the Charleston environment, "Human/Nature" aimed for a wider relevance as well. The exhibition, which I organized with associate curator Roberta Kefalos, was imagined as a way of mapping the transactions between nature and culture in a specific environment with the idea that it might anticipate the artistic interpretation of other natural systems and their human communities. As curators, we sought to describe many aspects of the connection between people and their environment—historic and contemporary, social and personal, beneficent and destructive. Rather than conceptualizing nature and culture in terms of an obsolete, even harmful duality, we proposed looking at landscapes along a continuum: as more or less transformed by human activity. In so doing, we tried to visualize what environmental historians have been proposing of late: that what most of us call "nature" is at once more complex and more compromised than can be

contained in the notion of wilderness, with which it is often assumed to be synonymous. Very little of nature exists apart from human life and human intervention; it is a cultural creation. The built environment is clearly a human artifact and has been so for millenniums—even the primeval forest supposedly encountered by the early settlers in this country turns out to have been significantly and purposefully modified by American Indians. To the extent that we are able to find places unchanged by human activity, the ways we see and describe them are still a projection of our attitudes and values. There is certainly a nature out there—and in us—but the ways we know it and the meanings we ascribe to it are all a function of our cultural imaginings.[1]

The close relationship between nature and culture prompted the project's purposefully ambiguous title. The term "human nature" denotes a set of psychological and social characteristics that distinguish the species: the impulse to find shelter and food, the desire to create families and communities, and the capacity to cope with disaster and death. Human nature also embraces more destructive forces: the instinct to kill, for example, or the impulse to exploit one another and our common natural resources—the latter made possible by the tendency to see both nature and what have come to be called "native peoples" as alien or exotic, rather than as distinct but interdependent parts of a dynamic system. All these human attributes contribute to the ways we inhabit a landscape. As used in the title, "human/nature" also alludes to the notion of reciprocity between culture and the environment. Landscapes are the outcome of a specific set of interactions between the species and the various biomes it inhabits. Nature shapes culture even as culture constructs

nature. Our landscapes express both human attributes and the interactions between humanity and the environment—that is, both "human nature" and "human/nature." It is these multiple meanings that the exhibition sought to explore. Some of the projects were as simple as marking a place in the landscape or making a frame for viewing the world, while others examined human behavior, history, race relations, cycles of growth and decay in nature and civilization, and attitudes to conflict or death.

Why use art to describe the connections between people and their environment? Contemporary culture in industrialized nations is struggling to shed attitudes of domination over nature that have created a legacy of wanton consumption, waste, unplanned sprawl, and pollution. At the same time, a burgeoning global population means that an ever-growing proportion of the environment is a cultural creation. Human impact on the environment is extending not only to the form of particular landscapes, but to the fate of whole ecosystems, to the distribution and extinction of species, even to global climate. As long ago as 1835, the noted Hudson River landscape painter Thomas Cole lamented what he called "the ravages of the axe": the felling of the great Catskill Mountain forests. "The most noble scenes are made desolate," he wrote in his "Essay on American Scenery," "and oftentimes with a wantonness and barbarism scarcely credible in a civilized nation. The way-side is becoming shadeless, and another generation will behold spots, now rife with beauty, desecrated by what is called improvement; which, as yet, generally destroys Nature's beauty without substituting that of Art." Just three decades later, the pioneering ecologist George Perkins Marsh insisted: "Man

has too long forgotten that the earth was given to him for usufruct alone, not for consumption, still less for profligate waste." Even then, Marsh felt, "The earth is fast becoming an unfit home for its noblest inhabitant."[2]

Our growing influence on planetary health makes the need for wise management ever more urgent. Mitigating human impact will require new paradigms in which ecology, history, social and environmental ethics, and esthetics might all coalesce. In the mind of the preeminent twentieth-century conservationist Aldo Leopold, environmental stewardship is at least in part an esthetic exercise, "the art of management...applied to land by some person of perception." Land-use questions, he insisted, should be examined "in terms of what is ethically and esthetically right, as well as what is economically expedient." To the extent that stewardship is an esthetic matter, art surely has a role to play in "preserving the integrity, stability, and beauty of the biotic community."[3] Art also has the capacity to articulate myths, even to shape them; there is some cause to hope that it might provide a model for reconciling cultural practice and environmental quality. While art is widely recognized to embody the ethos of a time and place, it can also—through a kind of cultural feedback—effect the larger patterns of social discourse. "Human/Nature" was intended as a contribution to the formation of some new cultural paradigms and as a way of helping to articulate both the ethics and the esthetics of land use. We hoped the exhibition would embody the delicate affinity between nature and artistic culture that characterizes the best aspects of the built environment, and to suggest that this rapport might be one of the cornerstones of environmental stewardship.

Unitarian Cemetery and Gateway Walk
between King and Archdale Streets

But why the need to commission these projects? Contemporary art is famous for its diversity, its forays into new media, and its embrace of unfamiliar subjects. Any one of these might have made for a good exhibition. But a show of commissioned projects aimed precisely at the intersection of nature and culture would underscore two of the most compelling developments in contemporary art: Much recent sculpture derives its power from a response to the particular circumstances of given environment—topography, social context, history. This contextualization generates both an especially satisfying art and a heightened experience of place. Coincident with this interest in place, more and more artists have focused their attention on landscape, creating their sculptures out-of-doors, shaping them from plants and earth, and subjecting them to the vagaries of weather and climate. This practice marks a sharp point of departure for artists, but it puts them closer to other partisans of nature—landscape architects, planners, garden designers, environmental activists, and ecologists.

The increasingly site-specific character of contemporary art has been the focus of numerous recent exhibitions, including the 1991 Spoleto Festival U.S.A. show of commissioned projects, "Places with a Past." But while that celebrated exhibition used the canvas of Charleston to reveal aspects of the city's history, the current project showed art created in response to the landscapes of the city and the surrounding low country. Inasmuch as landscape is a historical artifact, there were some inevitable areas of overlap between the two exhibitions. But "Human/Nature" featured a larger proportion of outdoor projects than "Places with a Past" and was attuned to culture chiefly as revealed by landscape rather than by architecture or by political history. Like "Places with a Past," "Human/Nature" explored the benefits of temporary projects—eleven out of the twelve installations were intended from the outset to be impermanent, which allowed the artists to be more experimental, even provocative, than they might have been with permanent commissions.

"Human/Nature" had several concurrent agendas. First, it addressed one of the festival's larger objectives: the ambition to become more inclusive. By commissioning projects for neighborhoods outside of the city center, the exhibition extended Spoleto's reach into communities not generally served by its programs, attracting new audiences. By increasing its involvement with visual culture, "Human/Nature" also made the festival more inclusive of all the arts. In the spirit of all of Spoleto's programs, "Human/Nature" was international in scope, affirming especially Charleston's historic links with Europe and Africa; and its artists ranged from well-established to newly emerging talents. The participants in "Human/Nature" also needed to meet curatorial objectives: They were selected for a demonstrated interest in landscape, either as a natural system or a social space. They were chosen with the expectation that they could respond to the landscape of the low country, interpreting the qualities of the natural environment and its layers of cultural history. Some of the selections may seem unusual to those familiar with the current crop of environmental artists. While a number of the participants frequently work in the landscape, others were making their first outdoor projects: The exhibition aimed to enlarge the pool of artists recognized for their interest in nature. It also aspired to a wide range of media, including video, because our experience of landscape is increasingly mediated by technology. We often come to know a landscape through photography and film, even through theme-park simulations.

To present the artists's projects in this volume, the Spoleto Festival U.S.A. commissioned noted landscape photographer Len Jenshel to document the works. His photography became an unplanned thirteenth project for "Human/Nature," as he also used his time in Charleston to pursue the vivid portrait of the low country that is presented as a companion to these essays. Jenshel was no stranger to the region: He had previously worked at Cypress Gardens and Middleton Place. Now he captured some of the area's other landmarks, such as Drayton Hall and Magnolia Plantation. He photographed the city from the water; he explored some of its historic gardens and burial grounds; he visited the marshes and beaches of the coastal islands. He also recorded some aspects of the local landscape less obviously picturesque: He was captivated by the flourishing ports facility; by the old Citadel (erected in the wake of Denmark Vesey's aborted 1822 slave rebellion) and the new (scene of protracted conflicts over the admission of women); and by the military presence that was long the lifeblood of the Charleston economy, which lingers in museumlike displays of cannons, warships, and helicopters at Patriots Point.

Jenshel even took aim at some truly offbeat subjects: a beach-in-the-making at a new resort across the Cooper River in Mt. Pleasant; a roofless warehouse—now a parking lot—on Bedon's Alley; and the city's streets, flooded by nine inches of rain early one summer morning. Above all, he captured a city in transition, as exemplified in so many ways: by the old Citadel, now a hotel catering to the

booming tourist trade, or by the facade of a nineteenth-century rice mill propped up forlornly in a sea of new BMWs, a relic of past industry awaiting some new use amid the stylish emblems of contemporary commerce. Thanks to Jenshel, this book is much more than a document of an event in Spoleto's 1997 season. It expresses an artistic imagination all its own, recording not only the photographer's responses to the projects in "Human/Nature," but also his interpretation of the coastal South Carolina landscape.

As revealed in Jenshel's photographs, Charleston affords exceptional opportunities for the kind of artistic exploration represented by "Human/Nature." Its natural setting and subtropical climate create an environment that is spectacular and diverse, encompassing ocean, estuaries, and rivers; cypress swamps and saltwater marshes; and maritime forests of pine, palmetto, and live oak. It is a place at once shaped and destroyed by its topography and climate: Built on a peninsula between two rivers, Charleston is subject to periodic earthquakes and all-too-regular hurricanes and floods. Its cultural landscapes are equally varied. Charleston has been home to numerous groups, including American Indians, Caribbean planters, English settlers, African slaves, and successive waves of French Huguenot, Jewish, Irish, and German immigrants. As one of the major ports of entry for slaves, Charleston has always had a substantial African-American population, which continues to be true to this day.

The legacy of cultural diversity is visible in the low-country landscape, which includes American Indian shell mounds and African-American yard art; public parks and lush private gardens in a variety of styles; Revolutionary and Civil War fortifications, picturesque cemeteries, waterfront promenades, and historic plantations. Although Charleston is most familiar for its historic district downtown, the city takes in the business and industrial area to the north, including a port facility now the third largest on the east coast. Charleston includes some places that are still rural, but also areas off-limits to habitation because of industrial pollution. Daniel Island, just across Cooper River from downtown, supplies a microcosm of these landscapes. Recently annexed by the city to provide it with growing room, it encompasses pristine saltwater marshes, agricultural lands, new housing constructed along neotraditional lines meant to evoke the old downtown neighborhoods; and vast impoundments of silt dredged from the rivers in an effort to keep shipping channels open.

The low country is a landscape of subtle charms rather than overt drama. It is characterized by quiet marshes, tidal estuaries, low dunes, and beaches. Its appeal comes from the lushness and variety of its vegetation, its extended growing season, and its pervasive gardens. Outwardly discreet, the landscape masks extremes of beauty and terror. Hidden in the loveliest places are narratives of horror: Some of the region's most beautiful gar-

Barracks at the Citadel

Estuary at the end of Fairchild Street
Daniel Island

Dredging pond
Daniel Island

dens were created by forced labor. Its peaceful cypress swamps, now refuges for alligators, egrets, and herons, were likewise built by slaves as freshwater impoundments for the cultivation of rice, which Africans were brought here to grow.

One of the oldest areas of New World settlement and colonization, the Charleston region has been the locus of more than three centuries of significant natural, social, and economic history. As told in fabulous detail by Theodore Rosengarten in his essay for this volume, Charleston was a center of pioneering efforts in botany, horticulture, and agriculture. The English naturalist Mark Catesby visited several times in the 1720s; the Philadelphia botanist John Bartram collected in the region in the 1760s; and Alexander Garden, a physician and gardener who was a correspondent with the Swedish botanist Carolus Linnaeus (and for whom the gardenia was named), lived in the city from 1752 until his death in 1791. Perhaps most famously, the

French explorer and naturalist André Michaux established a garden near Charleston in 1787 on commission from Louis XVI to collect New World flora that might have value to France. He also introduced many exotics: He is credited with bringing to America the fragrant tea olive, the crepe myrtle, the mimosa tree, the ginkgo, and—according to legend—the camellia. The French nurseryman Philippe Noissette and the American diplomat Joel Poinsett were also prominent in Charleston's botanical history; both have plants named for them: the class of roses known today as the noisettes, and the poinsettia.[4]

Botanical riches and a mild climate combined to endow Charleston with a significant garden tradition dating back to the colonial era. In the eighteenth century, imposing houses and gardens were created at plantations along the Ashley and Cooper rivers. Middleton Place, richly described in Rosengarten's text, lies 12 miles up the Ashley; it is justly famous for its curving terraced

lawns, butterfly lakes, axial walks, reflecting pools, and geometric parterres. Begun in the 1740s and designed in the grand manner derived ultimately from aristocratic French gardens, Middleton is one of the oldest surviving designed landscapes in America. Just down the river from Middleton is still more ancient Magnolia Plantation, established in the 1680s; its original house and most of its formal gardens are gone. The present gardens were laid out in the first half of the nineteenth century in a more informal picturesque manner with winding paths, serpentine lakes, and exotic trees and shrubs. Promoted today as "the complete plantation experience," Magnolia is one of the region's most popular tourist destinations, welcoming more than 150,000 visitors each year.

In the city itself, gardens are smaller and more intimate on the Anglo-Dutch model. They are generally enclosed with masonry walls and wrought iron gates; their symmetrical designs incorporate rectangular or square

Garden at William Gibbes House
South Battery

Clorenda's Exquisite Hair Design
Spring Street

beds bordered with brick and edged with box-wood; pavers of cobblestone or old brick; simple parterres; and sometimes topiary. This is the distinctive Charleston style, reinforced in the twentieth century by the New York landscape architect Loutrel Briggs, a winter resident beginning in 1927 who restored some historic gardens and created others in a historicist manner, as at the William Gibbes House on South Battery Street. Briggs was also involved in the design of Charleston's Gateway Walk, a quiet ramble off the city streets that opened in 1930, connecting several notable churches, gardens, and cemeteries in the heart of town. Charleston's active and influential preservation community insures the perpetuation of the local garden tradition today both at private homes and at public buildings throughout the city.

This is the privileged history of Charleston gardens, but it is by no means the only one. Kitchen gardens are found in the less fancy parts of town, along with more off-beat yards incorporating Astroturf or plastic plants. The city can even boast some full-blown examples of the African-American yard show, those intricate displays of paintings, root sculptures, and found objects such as bottles and mirrors, scrap metal and lumber, hubcaps, fans, and dolls found across the South. One such dressed yard was documented by Charleston writer Josephine Humphreys for the *New York Times Magazine* in 1989.[5] Though this particular garden is now gone, popular art is still in evidence in the city, as discovered by Len Jenshel at Clorenda's Exquisite Hair Design on Spring Street. While "Human/Nature" included a project inspired by Charleston's formal garden tradition, it also embraced the bottle trees and yard art of its less celebrated vernacular spaces.

In order to interpret such a wide range of environments, "Human/Nature" assembled a diverse group of artists from the region, the United States, Europe, and South Africa. Many were sculptors but others were landscape architects, painters, or video artists; some were academically trained but others were self-taught; some were engaged with high-art concerns, while others expressed popular or vernacular impulses. On one level, this variety was meant to break down some obsolete boundaries in the art world. In an ever more globalized and media-drenched culture, previously distinct cultural groups have begun to be more aware of each other, to overlap, to hybridize, and sometimes—less productively—to be thrown into conflict. Sculptors have become increasingly active in roles traditionally assigned to landscape architects, while landscape architects are increasingly inspired by contemporary sculpture, both as a three-dimensional articulation of space and as a source of symbolic form. Self-taught artists are winning a place in the broader art world: Many of their concerns and styles, often derived from popular culture, are being embraced—even mimicked—by academically trained ones. This hybridization has implications beyond the art world, however. Our goal in "Human/Nature" was not to present pluralism for its own sake, but to give voice to the competing racial, economic, and cultural groups that have given shape over the centuries to the landscapes of the low country. At the same time, the range of nationalities, styles, and points of view were intended to demonstrate how broadly the commitment to landscape has spread among contemporary artists in this environmentally conscious age. Landscape is one of the few things we all share, both as a set of natural resources that make life possible and as a significant locus of social interaction.

"Human/Nature" was more than a year in the making. Planning commenced in the spring of 1996; the artists began visiting Charleston in the fall to tour the city and the nearby countryside. They were given the broadest possible range of opportunities both with respect to site and subject. They identified the places where they wanted to work and spent the winter developing their proposals, while the festival staff secured the necessary permissions from public and private property owners. In two cases, the artists elected to bring existing work to Charleston. The internationally renowned Polish sculptor Magdalena Abakanowicz had recently completed a group of large and imposing bronze *Hand-like Trees*, which resemble both tree trunks and clenched or truncated hands. Because of the analogies they suggest between the body and plant life, the artist felt they were closely consistent with the themes of "Human/Nature" and proposed installing them on the high seawall at the Battery, the tip of the Charleston peninsula. Standing against the backdrop of sky and water, they evoked for many viewers both wind-damaged trees and wounded torsos. Meanwhile, Thornton Dial, a self-taught African-American artist, agreed to bring a group of sculptures from his yard show in Alabama and arrange them in one of the secret gardens at Middleton Place. Multicolored chairs and benches encrusted with roots and found objects formed the nucleus of his installation in Charleston, but he was so inspired by his visit to the city that he created a series of drawings and assemblages on local subjects—the revered octogenarian blacksmith Philip Simmons, sweetgrass basket weavers, and slave cabins at McLeod Plantation—that went on exhibition at the Gibbes Museum of Art.

Another project was already under way and received additional impetus from "Human/Nature." Portions of a garden featuring wrought iron by Philip Simmons had recently been completed at his church, St. John's Reformed Episcopal, and there were plans to extend it in his honor. Spoleto Festival U.S.A.'s support helped the Philip Simmons Foundation complete a whole new section behind the church, including a wall with double gates bearing a heart and cross motif. With the blessings of Simmons and his foundation, the festival was also able to engage the extraordinary South Carolina topiary artist Pearl Fryar to sculpt the plants for the garden. Fryar moved a large topiary suggesting interlocking hearts from his home in Bishopville, which is surrounded by fantastically shaped evergreens in free-form abstract shapes; he created others especially for the Philip Simmons garden. Working with the project's landscape architect, Sheila Wertimer, he also helped design and construct the garden's decorative walkways. Curiously, this was the project that most closely approached the Charleston garden tradition, though it was made by two self-taught artists. It was also the only installation intended from the outset to be permanent.

While the Philip Simmons garden was previously in the works, all the other projects came into being wholly in response to the festival's visual arts project. Several artists took their cues from historical landscapes. The New York sculptor Charles Simonds, for example, discovered a neglected grotto on the grounds of Ashley Hall School that he wanted to bring back to life. Working with students from the school, Simonds populated the interior with clay sculptures in human and animal shapes, reclaiming the grotto both as a social space and as an imaginative landscape.

At McLeod Plantation, a property of the Historic Charleston Foundation, landscape architect Martha Schwartz found her inspiration in a row of mid-nineteenth-century slave cabins under an allée of grand old oaks. Using long panels of white scrim and white grass paint, she created yards around each cabin that led across the axis of the oak trees into a field of sweetgrass, cultivated for the basketweavers still at work in Charleston. The resulting spaces were both hallowed and ghostly, but they offered a commentary on life and labor as well. They crossed—and interrupted—the dominant axis leading to the great house, connecting the slaves' modest dwellings with the site of their industry.

Others responded to apparently pristine, wild environments. On his visit to Charleston, the Dutch landscape architect Adriaan Geuze became enthralled with the cypress and sweetgum swamps at Magnolia Plantation and Cypress Gardens. He proposed building a garden room out over the black water, built of slender poles connected with wire that would be draped with Spanish moss. Approached by a boardwalk and containing a few simple benches, the pavilion was imagined as a meditative space in emulation of Japanese temple gardens. Cypress Gardens agreed to host the project in one of the region's naturalized wetlands created by slave labor in the eighteenth century as reservoirs for inland rice cultivation.

Sculptors Martha Jackson-Jarvis and Ronald Gonzalez both investigated the connections between landscape and spiritual life. Jackson-Jarvis, an African-American artist from Washington, D.C., who works in ceramic and Venetian tile, created a sculptural garden on Charleston's east side as an homage to Afro-Caribbean spiritual traditions and to the African-American experience of the coastal landscape. Gonzalez, a sculptor from Binghamton, New York, orchestrated a multipart installation that suggested that good and evil—both God and the devil—are still abroad in the landscape. At Magnolia Cemetery, a prime example of a nineteenth-century picturesque burial ground found on the north edge of Charleston, he installed a large assemblage of totemic figures and crosses in the open, while a group of angels took shelter in the cemetery gatehouse. The counterpart to these sanctified beings was found downtown, where numerous small devils made of cast and burned plaster, wax, paint, animal teeth, and bones infested a claustrophobic space at the Gibbes Museum of Art.

A renewed interest in landscape characterizes the work of artists in other media as well. Mary Lucier, for example, is a pioneer of video art whose compositions often contrast pristine landscapes with those that have suffered from human or natural disruption. For "Human/Nature," she created an evocative multimedia installation that featured video images projected on the four exterior walls of a small house built on stilts. Combining footage of actual storms with images taped indoors of actors in period dress at the historic Aiken-Rhett House, *House by the Water* suggested some of the imaginative links between social history and the elements.

"Human/Nature" even included a painted environment, created by Esther Mahlangu of South Africa. She is one of the foremost practitioners of Ndebele mural art, which emerged among the women of the tribe in the last several generations as a way of affirming cultural pride in the face of apartheid. With the help of her son, Elias, and his wife, Johanna, she transformed the entrance to the abandoned High School of Charleston to evoke the Ndebele homestead, in which portals and courtyards are painted in bright colors with motifs derived from nature and architecture. Mahlangu's project, like Simonds', affirms the potential of art to help restore our environment by bringing new life to old spaces.

"Human/Nature" also showcased the work of two environmental artists from the Southeast, Herb Parker and Patrick Dougherty. Parker, a sculptor who teaches at the College of Charleston, is known for organic architecture built of sod over a steel armature. For the Spoleto Festival U.S.A., he made a two-story colonnaded structure in White Point Garden, a public park at the Battery with a view out over the estuary. Dougherty, who lives in a handmade wooden house with a swept-dirt yard near Chapel Hill, works his magic with bundled maple saplings. He made a sculpture that was part shelter, part whirlwind, which lifted off from the sidewalk near City Hall, snaked through the trees and touched down inside Washington Park.

The projects are presented in this volume roughly as a visitor might have encountered them in Charleston, beginning at the Battery and White Point Garden, epicenter of the historic city, and moving up and off the peninsula. As different as they are from one another, the projects all partake of an age-old impulse that might itself fall into the category of behaviors known as human nature: the desire to make a differentiated, even consecrated, place for ourselves in the world. While they express a widespread phenomenon, they do so in response to a particular landscape: These artists all demonstrated a capacity to understand and address the specific geographic and social circumstances of Charleston. The works they contributed to "Human/Nature" were the catalysts for a series of genuine perceptual and emotional encounters with local history and cultural

traditions, along with the region's climate, topography, botany, and zoology. As such, they represented a suite of authentic experiences in an increasingly simulated world.

More generally, the projects presented in this book suggest the ways that art can help us fathom the complex interplay of natural and cultural forces that give shape to the environment. They assume their places along the continuum that bridges nature and culture, some of them subtle transformations of the environment while others are more emphatically human artifacts. Taken together, they suggest some of the ways that landscape art might help heal the breach between nature and culture. Once seen as a vast and inexhaustible other, nature is now being reconceived as a cultural creation. At one time perceived as essentially stable and unperturbable, nature is now recognized as a dynamic but fragile system, the health of which is contingent on human wisdom. The artists in "Human/Nature" affirm the possibility of a beneficent relationship with nature. They suggest a new model for stewardship, in which esthetics and historical awareness might merge with environmental and social ethics. They offer the hope that our energies might be marshaled to correct, not to create, environmental problems, and that nurture might at long last replace dominion as the paradigm of human nature.

Notes

1. The anthology *Uncommon Ground: Toward Reinventing Nature*, William Cronon, ed., (New York: W.W. Norton & Co., 1995) provides a good overview of the evolving perception of nature as a cultural construction; see also Alexander Wilson, *The Culture of Nature: North American Landscape from Disney to the Exxon Valdez* (Cambridge: Blackwell, 1992). On the American Indian

transformations of the precolonial landscape, see William Cronon, *Changes in the Land: Indians, Colonists, and the Ecology of New England* (New York: Hill and Wang, 1983).

2. Thomas Cole, "Essay on American Scenery" (1835), reprinted in John W. McCoubrey, *American Art 1700-1960* (Englewood Cliffs: Prentice Hall, 1965), 98-110; quotations are from p. 109. George Perkins Marsh, *Man and Nature* (1864; reprint ed., Cambridge: Belknap Press of Harvard University Press, 1965), 36, 43.

3. Aldo Leopold, "The Conservation Esthetic," in *A Sand County Almanac* (Oxford and New York: Oxford University Press, 1949; reprint ed. 1989), 175; and "The Land Ethic," ibid., 224-25.

4. For more on Charleston's role in botanical exploration, see James R. Cothran, *Gardens of Historic Charleston* (Columbia: University of South Carolina Press, 1995). This book is also a good source for an amplification of the city's garden history given in the next paragraph.

5. African-American gardens range from the purely functional to the elaborately dressed. For those at the more utilitarian end of the spectrum, see Richard Westmacott, *African-American Gardens and Yards in the Rural South* (Knoxville: University of Tennessee Press, 1992); for those at the more elaborate end, see Robert Farris Thompson, "The Song that Named the Land: The Visionary Presence of African-American Art" in *Black Art—Ancestral Legacy: The African Impulse in African-American Art* (Dallas: Dallas Museum of Art, 1989), 123-35. For the Charleston example, see Josephine Humphreys, "Inhabited by History: Charleston, S.C.," *New York Times Magazine/The Sophisticated Traveler* (March 12, 1989), 32.

Overleaf:
St. John's Lutheran Cemetery
Archdale and Clifford Streets

Mrs. PAMELIA S. ADAIR
Wife of
CAPT. W. E. ADAIR
Died on the 22nd July 1861

In the Master's Garden

By Theodore Rosengarten

The river wants straining,
and the land draining,
to make either of them
properly wet or dry.
—*Fanny Kemble Butler*

Crossing the Gulf Stream on their voyage to the province of Carolina, the French Protestant refugees of 1682 must have sensed they were approaching a continent. Rafts of seaweed, layered with debris from coastal vegetation, and the myriad birds and creatures who feed around the detritus, glided northerly on warm eddies. The water was a brilliant blue color. A unity of wind and current pushed against His Majesty's ship, *The Richmond*, from the southwest. Schools of jellyfish known as Portuguese man-of-wars, their sail-like sacs raised out of the water as if to catch the breeze, drifted and fished in the robust American stream.

Another day of good sailing and the Huguenots would glimpse the hazy tree line on the western horizon. They had heard about the endless Carolina forest, a forest older and taller than any in England or France, a forest that did not belong to a king. Soon they would lie outside the bar at Charles Towne, in sight of thickets of colossal oak trees with curiously twisted boughs and soldierly palmettos, topped with hats of leafy fronds, standing at ease at their beach posts. Disembarking at a wharf on the east side of the island-shielded peninsula, the immigrants collected provisions for the short journey north to the Santee River. Lured by the promise of fertile land and the opportunity to worship freely, they thought they would support themselves by supplying England and its colonies with foods such as wine and olive oil that Europeans were used to.

The ship's clerk lingered a year in the vicinity of Charles Towne. On his return to England, he published a description of the province with an account of its history and the outlook for getting rich. A cross between a real estate prospectus and a travelogue, Thomas Ashe's report was directed at the reader whose birth, in the words of an earlier promoter, Robert Horne, "has not entitled him to any of the Land of his ancestors, yet his Industry may supply him so, as to make him the head of as famous a family." Ashe painted a rosy picture of life on the planta-

Grass terraces and Butterfly Lakes seen over Rice Mill Pond

Middleton Place

tions newly laid out on the banks of the Ashley and Cooper rivers. Brimming with an optimism grounded in the latitudinal thinking of his day which placed Carolina in a belt with "those Delicious countries about Aleppo, Antioch, and Smyrna," as Horne had called them, as well as "the Province of Nanking, the richest in China," Ashe invoked the image, later appropriated by the conquerors of India, of "a Jewel to the Crown of England."

The biggest surprise in this land of wonders was that, in the two decades since William Hilton had sounded the waters and measured the land, more people had not taken advantage of the opportunity to own a piece of the Jewel. From the headway made by Old World plants and animals, especially weeds and disease-carrying microbes, it can be said that the biological conquest of Carolina was well under way, yet with little direct human effort. Ashe solves the mystery of low European numbers by noting the colonists' failure to discover a plausible staple crop—a food, drug, or fiber that could fill a steady demand abroad and create quick wealth.

Rice was still ten years away. Indigo was tried and dropped and would not be planted commercially until the middle of the eighteenth century. It would be 110 years before long-staple cotton triumphed on the Sea Islands of Georgia and South Carolina. In the meantime, there was no sugar crop to sweeten the puddings and pies of London and Paris, no tobacco to feed Europe's passionate addiction. Kept out of these markets more by the politics of empire than by the constraints of nature, the planters of Carolina built a modest wealth by harvesting the woods and supplying meat to other parts of the Indies. Cattle turned into the forests, marshes, and swamps needed no fodder, hence no expenditure of the planter's scarce labor. "An ox," observed a traveler, "is raised at almost as little expense in Carolina as a hen is in England." Pigs put out to roam fattened on mast and acorns, then were penned and gorged on Indian corn before going to market.

In an era when "the limitations of the tree proved the limitations of the ship," the forests of the Carolina coastal plain beckoned naval architects and the barons of commerce who dreamed of dominating the sea. Planters sent squads of servants and slaves to collect the resinous juice of the longleaf pine and boil it down to make pitch and tar for caulking and preserving the wooden ships that were transforming the once-formidable ocean into a land bridge. Longleaf pines whose trunks shoot up straight with no branches for fifty or sixty feet were cut down for masts, while the great live oaks yielded planking and curved pieces called compass timbers for catheads, knees, and sterns.

To promoters like Thomas Ashe, meat and forest products signified a passing stage in the development of the province. Unimpressed by the landscape of agricultural production, Ashe was struck by the spectacle of gardens. After ten years of struggling to regulate the food supply, planters had begun to plant for "ornament" and "pleasure" as well as for "use." They "beautified" and "adorned" the grounds with "Flowers which to the Smell or eye are pleasing and agreeable," such shapely, fragrant invaders as the rose, domesticated by ancient peoples in Asia and Europe; the tulip, of Near Eastern ancestry, and by 1630 a thriving Dutch export; the carnation, a Eurasian perennial in the pink family; and the "Lilly," ideal for perennial borders, available in varieties for every extreme of sun and shade, from growers in England, Holland, and France. Not only in their self-interested search for a staple but in their avocational gardening, Carolina's early planters carried on a global exchange of seeds and plant stocks.

Through the 1690s and the rush to clear the inland swamps for rice, plantation gardens differentiated into sundry forms—sumptuous gardens designed by specialists from Europe and installed over years by gangs of slaves; informal, naturalistic gardens chiseled out of the indigenous woods; allées or walks between rows of evenly spaced trees; kitchen gardens, adjacent to freestanding cookeries, supplying vegetables for the master's larder and medicinal, savory, and aromatic herbs; slave gardens, up to a half-acre per black household, intensively planted with roots, tubers, leafy vegetables, and spices, and bordered with flowering shrubs whose exuberance would have been out of place in the master's domain; beds and yard gardens dedicated to the planter's wife who may have tended them herself and used them for naturalizing foreign plants or for raising a crop of groundnuts, melons, or exotic vegetables; greenhouses and experimental plots where the planter propagated seeds and cuttings.

Each garden type had a defined area and an inventory of plants, and each signified a set of values and ideals. The formal gardens showed off the planter's wealth but also his desire for a place in the traditional hereditary aristocracy with its yearning for comfort, its acceptance of responsibility for taming the wild, and its wish to create a work of art on the land. Slave gardens routinely exceeded the utilitarian purposes for which they were set aside, becoming focal points of unslavelike feelings of ownership and spaces for working out continuities with African esthetic principles. Taken together, the effect of these many kinds of gardens was not the imposition on the earth of a single notion of order but rather what, in another context, architectural historian Vincent Scully has called "a vast release, not only of the human spirit, which is liberated into space, but of some great order within the earth itself, now made visible, freed."

Gardening preceded staple-crop agriculture in the low country and has outlasted it, too. While the gardens that once provided food have been covered over by epochs of vegetation, the renovated gardens of well-to-do planters are shrines in today's tourist landscape. The most impressive of these can be found in what South Carolina historian Henry Savage has termed "that rich area haunted by Catesby and other naturalists, the shores of the Ashley River." In fact, the Ashley is a short, shallow river, with no important sources of fresh water. Hardly ideal for rice, the river might more accurately be called an arm of the sea, for it rises and falls simultaneously with the tide in the harbor. Yet the bluffs of the Ashley attracted Europeans to whom every inch of altitude was precious. Sir John Yeamans procured a boatload of slaves from Barbados in 1671—the first recorded entry of Africans into the province—to clear his new plantation on the Ashley. Mark Catesby, who spent the winter of 1723-24 around Charles Towne, collecting material for his *Natural History of Carolina, Florida, and the Bahama Islands*, took time to lay out the avenue of oaks at the Bull family seat at Ashley Hall. In 1741, the first Henry Middleton acquired lands on the Ashley by marrying Mary Williams, daughter of John and Mary Baker Williams. Middleton's slaves impounded wetlands at the foot of the bluff for rice, but for the next ten years the major work of the plantation was the construction of some 60 acres of formal gardens.

What the great French historian Marc Bloch said about the fate of manuscripts pertains to gardens too. Their experiences as objects are interesting in themselves because they conform to the vicissitudes of life. Survivors of two wars and a powerful earthquake, and almost alone in resisting the post-Revolutionary movement to dig up formal gardens and replace them with imitations of nature, the gardens of Middleton Place are an outstanding site for contemplating how people change the earth and are themselves changed in the process.

Charles Towne's siren song tempted the restless and disenfranchised of northern Europe. Besides the Huguenots came groups of English dissenters, French- and German-speaking Swiss, Scotch-Irish Presbyterians, Gaelic-speaking highlanders, commerce-minded lowlanders, Welsh Baptists, Lutherans, Quakers, German Reformed, Sephardic Jews—some coming to blend and build a new polity with others, but most hoping to establish communities of co-religionists based on land-ownership, agricultural self-sufficiency, and trade. Provincial authorities, hoping to expand Charles Towne's lines of communication and to defend the colony against the incursions of hostile Indians and foreign rivals such as Spain and mischievous New England, sent many would-be settlers to live on the frontiers. People of every nationality set up shop and household in town, so that at the time Henry Middleton was constructing his global garden on the Ashley, Charles Towne was the most linguistically diversified spot in Britain's Atlantic empire, "for its sources of population," explained historical geographer D. W. Meinig, "stretched from Scotland to Mozambique."

The leading source of people after 1708 was Africa. The need for labor on the new rice plantations could not be met by the supply of indentured Europeans. Transported in the vicious commerce prosaically called the slave trade, Africans instantly monopolized the role of field hand. Contemporary reports and evidence unearthed by archeologists suggest the extent to which the countryside was Africanized. The majority of people lived in small, windowless, clay-walled houses with split-planked roofs covered with palmetto thatch. Open hearths on dirt floors provided heat in winter and a defense against mosquitoes in summer. Historian Peter Wood quotes a Swiss settler in 1737 who remarked that "Carolina looks more like a negro country than a country settled by white people."

Even Charles Towne, with its "tree-shaded streets of large, closely set Georgian houses with their West Indian piazzas," was decidedly African in its sounds and social patterns. Most of its residents, whether servants in the grand homes, or laborers, seamen, or renegades lodged in the outlying neighborhoods, were black. They lived in open disregard of a slave code that no one had a stake in enforcing. "In human terms," Meinig concludes, with sweeping precision, "Charles Towne might best be described as the capital of an African foothold with a diverse minority of Europeans all under the shaping influence of English West Indian experience, forcibly wedged into American Indian realms."

But where were the American Indians, offspring of the people who greeted William Hilton and whetted his appetite with their fat crops of corn? How is it that they so conveniently departed, as if by mutual agreement, to make way for the newcomers from across the sea? We must not assume that they disap-

Overleaf:
**East Battery Street from
Charleston Harbor**

peared as meekly from the land as they have from our history books, or that their demise was inevitable, that things could have turned out no other way. Had Hilton made contact two centuries earlier, he likely would have encountered a much larger Indian population, as yet untouched by Old World diseases. A hundred years earlier, he might have found fewer people than he met in 1663, for the coastal peoples in the sixteenth century were visited again and again by the same lethal illnesses that were decimating natives of the Indies and Florida.

The Indians, by their own telling, had been much reduced from a peak population in antiquity. But what Hilton reported was evidence of demographic recovery. Furthermore, relations between the Indians and Hilton's followers reveal differences in ways of relating to the land and to one another that seem complementary and surmountable. The Indians described in seventeenth-century English narratives from Carolina had already undergone extensive cultural change.

The spectacular period of mortality from disease among the coastal American Indians may have ended fifty years before Hilton arrived. How many people died in the first waves of viral and bacterial invasion? If the Indians who greeted Hilton were indeed a remnant, how large was the whole cloth? We don't know. In the absence of written records for Carolina in the sixteenth century, when the Indians first encountered French and Spanish explorers, the best we can do to answer these questions is to extrapolate from the experience of Florida, where the Spanish kept detailed records of the chronology and impact of Old World diseases. Lacking immunity to the pathogens that stole aboard every ship and were present at every human encounter, from

American Indian mound
Magnolia Plantation

a handshake to sexual intercourse, the Indians of Florida succumbed to one disease after another in periodic epidemics of plague, smallpox, typhus, measles, mumps, influenza, and gastrointestinal and respiratory infections. Each new disease attacked a wholly susceptible population, a "virgin soil," so to speak, since surviving smallpox, for example, did not confer immunity to the flu. Geographer Henry Dobyns estimates that the native peoples had declined by ninety percent after seventy-five years of contact.

By the time the first Englishmen set foot in Carolina and wrote about it, the situation had dramatically improved. Hilton reported, "The Natives are very Healthful; we saw many Aged among them." Reaching old age was a good indicator of health. Of course, Hilton was trying to persuade Englishmen to emigrate, and his purpose must have colored his perceptions. Yet the English writers were all in agreement: The Indians of Carolina appeared healthy. While the founders of New England had marveled, forty years before, at the sickliness of the Indians and interpreted their elimination as a sign of God's good will toward the English, the promoters of England's southernmost province emphasized the natives' well-being. Thomas Ashe wrote that the Indians were good physicians, by which he meant they had an extensive understanding of medicinal plants, and their medicine worked. He would not have known, and we cannot be certain, if the Indians had learned to combat disease by adopting European ideas of contagion, quarantine, and nursing as almost certainly happened in Florida.

The Indians' accommodation to knowledge that Europeans had gained in the health calamities of the Middle Ages was a form of cultural change that can be inferred but not

proved by the historical record. There can be no doubt, however, about the reality of other cultural changes. The Indians Hilton conversed with had a larger French and Spanish vocabulary than he did. They were familiar with guns, and were no more "startled at the firing of a Peece of Ordnance" than he was. They preferred iron tools to the wood, bone, and shell implements their technology could produce. They built houses with squared timbers, showing their skills with iron. Though the deer of the wild were their cattle, some small Indian groups, excluded perhaps from the better hunting grounds, had begun herding cattle and hogs, courtesy of their trade with New England, before Hilton ever sailed from Barbados.

The chief signs of human recovery were the fields and granaries bursting with corn. The cultivators of this bounty were not a people in the midst of upheaval. They were secure and capable enough to raise food for a large population. English eyes beheld the harvest but not the achievement. Though "the Land be overgrown with weeds through their laziness," Hilton commented, as much on a moral flaw in the Indians as on the fertility of the soil, "yet they have two or three Crops of corn a year." Elsewhere, he remarked that they "plant in the worst Land, because they cannot cut down the timber in the best." Imagine, he teased his readers, what the best land, cleared of the valuable timber, would produce. Lacking the know-how, tools, and will to fell the biggest trees, the Indians held the land for a lower purpose. "Yet," Hilton admits, ignoring the absurdity of the paradox, "they have plenty of corn, Pumpions, Watermellons, Musk-mellons. . . ."

If he had stopped to ask himself how a lazy, technologically backward people could

American Indian mound
Magnolia Plantation

produce all that they needed to feed themselves and to feed him, too, he would have answered, "the Land," which he compared to the most productive soils of the bounteous Indies. Philosophically committed to a market economy as the arbiter of morality, he could not imagine that people might willingly limit agricultural production to what was required to live and to sustain the land so it would go on producing. Accumulating wealth by growing the largest crop they could and exchanging it for money was not their objective.

Hilton did appreciate the Indians' practice of burning the forest understory to create openings for game and to generate new vegetation for deer. The Indians may have burned the woods for other reasons, too, such as eliminating cover for their enemies and promoting the growth of food-bearing trees. Whatever the reasons for their reliance on fire, the Indians' forestry methods yielded what whites wanted: game for meat, skins, and fur. By 1682, "all the Considerable Planters" had their own Indian hunters who, for the paltry sum of twenty shillings a year, would "feed a family of thirty people with as much Venison and Fowl as they can well eat." So long as Indian hunters brought in commodities that were useful to the Europeans, their presence just beyond the plantation district was tolerated.

Twelve years into the slow process of settling Europeans in Carolina, Ashe boasted the Indians were "so thin of people" from fighting one another, that the English were "already too strong for all the Indians within five hundred miles" of Charles Towne. His boast was thirty years premature, but his confidence in the end result was not misplaced. Nothing the Indian agronomists had achieved gave them rights to the land. They were forced not merely to change, which they had shown they

could, but to relinquish their place on the land and to serve the usurpers, as hunters and guides, as cheap labor, but mainly as producers of deerskins for the Charles Towne trade. It made no difference, contends Charles Hudson, the foremost historian of the Southeastern Indians, what the native people of Carolina may have believed was the proper relationship of man to nature. Their beliefs bore little connection to what they had to do to survive. They slaughtered deer to the point of scarcity, and they fought and enslaved one another "because of their position on the outer fringes of an expanding world-system."

Questions about numbers, such as how many Indians were living in the low country or visiting seasonally at the time of the English invasion, or how many were here 170 years earlier when the Spanish made contact with the people of the Caribbean and Mesoamerica, are of more than antiquarian interest. A high population density would indicate a hierarchical society based on extensive agriculture. These people would have spent most of the year in one place, a prerequisite, wrote South Carolina novelist William Gilmore Simms, for "civilization." It would challenge the myth of the wilderness, since Europeans and Africans would have been moving onto land that was more "widowed" than wild. It would throw into sharp contrast the American Indians' failure to reproduce under the pressures of European avarice with the relative reproductive success of Africans on old Indian lands. Only in that part of the American mainland under English rule did African numbers grow by natural increase during the era of slavery. Everywhere else in the New World, the supply of African workers had to be replenished continuously through imports, prolonging the misery of Africa and

drawing into the slave trade millions of souls who would not bear children or whose children would not reach child-bearing age. Thus the reproductive success of Africans in the American South was exceptional, while the experience of Africans elsewhere in the Americas was closer to that of the native peoples they supplanted.

I live 7 miles from the Santee River where, in the 1680s, the Huguenots planted their first crops—Old World varieties of grapes and olives that failed to meet expectations. But the rice that was introduced here a decade later, and the cotton that transformed the lower reaches of the river, were the finest the world has ever seen. These great staples are no longer grown here, but descendants of the people who cultivated them are still around. One of my neighbors, the late York McGinnis, planted a quarter-acre of rice on a piece of moist low ground until about 1980. A man of 80 when I met him, he worked his crop with an old-fashioned, African-style, long-handled hoe, and he prepared the rice using the same basic tools slaves had used three hundred years ago, tools such as gourds for measuring and pouring, flails for threshing the seeds off the stalks, mortars and pestles for milling and polishing, and winnowing baskets for separating the chaff from the valuable grain.

Actually, Mr. York's baskets were broken and his failing sight discouraged him from gathering the material to repair them. So he used an old washpan to fan his rice when it came out of the mortar. Just as he did when he used a fanner basket, he called up the wind with a song. When he finished cleaning enough rice for our dinner, he turned

Cypress Gardens

the washpan over and showed me how it took the shape of the sky from horizon to horizon. (The fanner basket has better contours.) People came into the world, he said, through an opening in the sky. I was not sure if he was relating how people from Africa came to the Santee or if he was making a more general statement. I was beginning to see, however, that a technology so plain in appearances could be rich in meaning, whether or not the meaning was clear to me. And that Mr. York believed his ancestors had always grown rice, regardless of where they lived. What slavery had done, if he was right, was to introduce the element of compulsion and alter the scale of work.

In fact, the work that went into reshaping the environment in order to grow wet-culture rice can only be imagined. Swamps had to be diked to separate land from water. On some plantations, earth for the continuous levee parallel to the source of fresh water, a bank as tall as a person and 15 feet wide at the base, was wheeled to the site from distant clay pits. The outside wall held back the tides while the workers felled the cypress and gum trees, magnolias and tupelos, and water-tolerant oaks. Then the swamp floor was cleared and chiseled with hoes until it was as level as a billiard table. A network of inner crossbanks was thrown up to divide the land into 20-acre fields, also called squares. Canals and ditches leading to trunks—at first, literally hollowed-out logs—with hanging doors which opened and closed with the changing tides, carried fresh water onto and off the fields. A single rice plantation contained several miles of banks, and four times as many miles of canals and drains, all built and maintained with simple hand tools and a minimum of animal power.

These earthworks have left a profound mark on South Carolina's wetlands and have endowed the state with thousands of acres of genuine ruins. The rice planters were not thinking about building monuments, but what they left behind *is* monumental—sculptural earthen grids capable of evoking man's temporal conquest of nature, and nature's ultimate conquest of man. Now the rivers are reclaiming them, slowly but surely.

From the first sprouting of the rice seed that probably came from the East African island of Madagascar, where the British enjoyed a brief monopoly on the slave trade, to the production of some eighty million pounds of grain on the eve of the Civil War, growers were perpetually looking for ways to increase the work performed by water. They wanted to send water onto their fields *when* they wanted it, and their agricultural innovations sought freedom from nature's clock. By 1710, Carolina rice was being touted in London as the best in the world. As fine and profitable as they were, the first commercial crops planted on low ground and irrigated by rain and natural flooding were subject to parching drought. Sowing rice in the cleared inland swamps gave planters access to more reliable sources of water from ponds and artificial reservoirs. Still, the impounded water was used only to moisten the ground and feed the growing rice plants. Though the yield per acre and per worker improved, here the problem was too much water, for the fields were periodically inundated by spring floods, or freshets. The move to the swamplands adjacent to the tidal rivers began in the 1750s and intensified after the Revolution. Now water could be let on and off the fields with forethought, and the water could be put to work cultivating as well as irrigating the crop. Planting was timed so

that water could be turned on the freshly sown field with the next tidal surge. This shallow flooding, called the "sprout" flow, stayed on the fields until the grain "pipped" in four or five days, when the water was drained off at low tide. Three more times the fields would be flooded and drained, followed by periods of drying and hoeing. The "point" or "stretch" flow stayed on as long as a week. It killed weeds and protected the tender plants from birds whose immense flocks darkened the sky when they took to flight. The fields steeped under the "long" flow for two weeks or more. This flooding, which came over the tops of the plants, killed insects and grasses that competed with the rice for a place in the soil. The water was lowered and kept at a level so that the tips of the plants were visible. In late summer, the "lay-by" or "harvest" flow, lasting up to eight weeks and creating a landscape of shimmering beauty, supported the rice stalks until the grain ripened and was "ready for the hook." Without the water to hold them up, the panicles of this horticulturally improved rice would fall over.

Planters varied the flooding routine by lengthening, shortening, adding, or eliminating certain flows according to local conditions. The most successful growers knew not only how to select good seed and get the most work out of their slaves, but how to tap effectively into the tidal source that pulsed up the rivers. By carefully observing the strength of the surge in different seasons and under different weather conditions, and by learning to read the river's surface to calibrate the level and mix of fresh water and salt, they coaxed the river to wash away the salts that had accumulated in the fields and to drop nutrient-rich silts gathered in runoffs upstream. In lieu of the costly or impossible alternative of cultivating

Pathway along a levee
Cypress Gardens

more acres, rice planters tried to maximize their incomes by maximizing the use of water.

Responding to falling yields on deteriorating soils, innovators in the generation before 1861 experimented with a system of "open trench" planting that substituted water for the soil as the sprouting medium. The seed would be rolled in clay and sown in trenches, which would be flooded without being covered by dirt. When it worked, this procedure prompted quick germination and rapid growth, shortening the growing season by two to three weeks. Grass, weeds, and volunteer rice—the planter's nemesis, sprouting from seeds left in the field by the previous crop—were sharply curtailed, and the labor saved by reducing the number of hoeings could be assigned to cleaning ditches and keeping the banks and floodgates in good repair.

If agricultural reform in the upland South transformed cotton and tobacco plantations into what Virginia planter Richard Eppes called "chemical laboratries," then technology had converted the rice plantations of the low country into what the Santee planter and historian David Doar called "hydraulic machines." In a little more than a century, planters and slaves disassembled the complex ecosystems of the rivers, redeployed wetlands behind earthen fortifications, separated and diverted the fresh water from the salt, and channeled the energy of the tides into grassy stalks bearing pearly white grains of rice.

Once the earthworks were raised, and a system of regulating the flow of water was in place, the workers settled into a life of drudgery producing rice and maintaining the plantation. Because the challenges of farming with water and processing the grain never let up, and because water, wind, and other natural forces are continually modeling the land, without regard to man's desires, growers periodically had to mobilize their hands to repair breaches in the banks or, if the threshing mill went down, for example, to beat the grain out of the husks of mountains of rice sheaves with flails—free-swinging sticks tied to the ends of long handles. Like sailors fighting to save their ship in a stormy sea, the rice slaves' interactions with nature required a high degree of regimentation and obedience to authority.

As in Asia, where farmers also had to bring water to their fields, the low-country elite resisted change, even after rice planting ceased and the basis of economic life shifted. Neither did the former slaves, now the menial social class, embrace full change from the past. The master class clung to its privileges in the form of race-based institutions, while the heirs of the slaves insisted on preserving the task system at the core of their labor arrangements.

The task system under slavery was a way of getting work done that was peculiar to rice and Sea Island cotton plantations. Each hand was required to complete a defined quantity of work in a day, the equivalent of hoeing one "task" of ground which, on established rice plantations, measured out to a half acre. For every job, the task was the same from one plantation to the next, and known to masters and slaves alike. The system left no room for misunderstanding. All the worker had to do was locate the task stakes in the field to know how much ground he had to hoe, or how much rice he had to cut. Tasks were set for threshing, pounding, and winnowing, and though the work was done under the direction of a driver who stood ready with a lash to hurry things along, a task was a limit, like a line drawn on the ground, which the worker knew he would not have to cross. With the introduction of horse-drawn plows and steam-powered mills into the rice routine, planters had to adjust tasks to accommodate hand work with the latest technologies.

Under the task system, the workday was divided into two parts—the master's time, which was spent attending to the staple crop or to other jobs, and the slaves' own time, which could be used for gardening, fishing, hunting; boat-, basket- and netmaking; spiritual activities, or relaxation. The meat and produce slaves raised after hours belonged to them, though the planter could appropriate the blades or leaves from their corn plants for fodder. Generally, the hands kept what they grew for their own use or to swap or sell. Thus, though their standard of living stayed unremittingly low, they acquired property and an attitude of ownership.

A feature of life under slavery and freedom, the task system may have had antecedents in Africa, which is not to say that it was carried over intact or that people clung to it from a sense of cultural necessity. The issue is part of the larger question of what Africans contributed to rice agriculture in the formative years of the plantations. Until recently, the question was not even asked, either because it was accepted that the brutal passage from Africa had wiped out the past or because Africans were dismissed as a barbarous people who helped build America with their muscles and not with their minds.

The book that broke the mold of this kind of thinking was Peter Wood's *Black Majority: Negroes in Colonial South Carolina from 1670 through the Stono Rebellion*. Wood suggests that Africans sold off ships in Charles Towne may have known more about growing rice than their buyers did. Rice was not grown in the British Isles, where most of the white people came from, but rice was cultivated in the coastal wetlands and inland

Bennett Rice Mill (1844) with new BMWs
State Ports Authority, Concord Street

deltas of West Africa. It was no coincidence that Africans known to have come from rice-growing areas commanded higher prices than people who came from other parts.

Wood's thesis marked a departure from both the benign view of the plantation as a school for primitives, and the view, reflecting recent European history, of the plantation as a concentration camp. Instead, Wood takes seriously the opinion of the planters themselves. It behooved them, they thought, to know something about the background of the people they were buying. Far from seeking ignorant, unskilled workers, they put a premium on Africans who may have cultivated rice. Following Wood, Daniel C. Littlefield asked why planters preferred slaves from certain African ethnic groups over others. In the records of slave ships and in newspaper advertisements for runaway slaves, merchants, ship captains, and planters compiled a veritable catalog of strengths and weaknesses, including judgments on character and work ethics associated with specific African peoples.

Could planters successfully predict that a person from the Gold Coast would make a better rice hand than someone from Angola? Was there any truth to their analysis of African emotional traits, or was it a list of fictions? We can say only that planters observed their workers closely, were aware of their individuality as well as their ethnicity, and respected their capacity to learn.

Many Africans had never seen a rice plant before coming to Carolina, but many others had. Africans who collaborated in the slave trade were provisioning slave ships with rice as early as 1600. African-American techniques such as covering the seed with the heel of the foot and winnowing with a fanner basket, calling the wind with a song and pounding rice in a mortar, were just like those found in Africa. Not all aspects of rice growing on the two continents were comparable, however. Carolina planters modified the environment to suit the crop, by moving earth and water. African growers relied, by and large, on natural flooding and altered their methods of farming rather than alter the land.

The impetus for making over the land came from Europeans. The world was their marketplace. They put up money, moved people, plants, animals, and commodities across an ocean, and made a lot more money. Carolina rice growers became, in fact, the wealthiest planter group in North America. They were specialists, and their numbers were limited. Of all of the South's old staple crops, rice was the most restricted by geography. Cotton could flourish in the uplands or the lowlands, but wet-culture rice was commercially viable only along a 5- to -20-mile stretch above salt water on the rivers between the Cape Fear, in North Carolina, and the St. Johns, in Florida. On ten rice rivers and their branches and tidal creeks, South Carolina produced the bulk of America's crop.

A decade after the American Revolution, when France and the West Indies were engulfed in violent upheaval, the South experienced a revolution in agriculture, also long-lasting in its consequences. The invention of an economical process for granulating sugar was bringing regimentation, wealth, and political power to the sugar parishes in the lower Mississippi. Improvements in flue-curing tobacco were restoring profits to Virginia's oldest industry. The fabrication of a rice-pounding mill by a machinist and windmill maker from Northumberland, England, enabled planters, for the first time, to mill as much grain as their hands could harvest. Planters on the Sea Islands of South Carolina solved the problem of adapting their salt-swept lands to a staple crop by tapping into an ecology whose primary plant, *Spartina* grass, had solved for itself the problems of growing in salt. They used the marsh grass and the marsh mud to feed a type of long-staple cotton introduced from the Near East, via Loyalists from Carolina who had resettled in the Indies. This black-seed variety yielded a strong and uncommonly fine fiber that made them wealthy overnight. The invention by a Connecticut Yankee vacationing in Georgia of a machine that cleanly separated cotton seeds from the lint ignited the expansion of short-staple cotton and the spread westward of the plantation way of life.

Meanwhile, Carolina's rice planters were quietly completing their move from the inland swamps to the tidal rivers. They moved into larger mansions, while their slaves moved out of their clay-walled huts into rough plank cabins, just as the log-trunks in the rice grids were replaced by plank culverts. With the end of the transatlantic slave trade in sight—the authors of the Constitution, not foreseeing the rise of cotton, set December 31, 1807, as the last day that African slaves could enter the country—knowledge of the slave's African background faded in importance, and the ethnic African was displaced in white awareness by the interchangeable Negro field hand.

In the heyday of rice before the Civil War, a respectable yield for each worker capable of completing a full task was four to five barrels, weighing five hundred pounds apiece, or the output of 2 acres—minus four to five bushels per barrel, or a steady fifteen percent of the crop, that was eaten by birds. But the birds, and the rats who also took a share, left

Loading a container ship at the State Ports Authority
Charlotte Street

more to the planter than he could process by the old hand methods. By the late 1830s, there began appearing on the landscape tall brick chimneys extending above the roofs of steam-powered threshing and pounding mills. Because they burned wood and other solid fuel, the mills did not have to be near the water, and the site of finishing the rice moved to higher and more solid ground. Milling by steam introduced new costs. It took about a cord of firewood to make a barrel of rice. Woodcutters were kept busy all year to meet the seasonal need of the boilers, and the forests shrank perceptibly. Some planters began specializing in milling rice for their neighbors, and some, to avoid the expense of building and operating a machine, shipped their rice in the rough to Charleston or directly to Europe, where mills had been erected to process the grain. Rice shipped better with the husk on, and planters were glad to be rid of the headaches of milling and packing.

I was shown around the gardens at Middleton Place by horticulturist Sidney Fraser and volunteer interpreter Merrill Robling. Fraser, a native of Johns Island, started out raking paths at Middleton twenty-five years ago. Today he is in charge of a staff of seven people who tend the 65 acres of formal gardens set against a backdrop of 6,500 acres of ponds, lawns, roads, woodlands, barnyards, and irrepressible natural vegetation that constitutes the historic landscape. Robling recently returned home to Charleston after spending most of her adult life in gray northern cities where her husband managed steel mills. Her years of exile, we joked, coincided with the disappearance of the color green from modern landscape painting.

We met at the portal to the gardens and walked through to the west side of a perfectly rectangular reflection pool that once went by the name "Long Lake." Two hundred yards long and 30 yards wide, the pool on its north side marks the boundary between the formal gardens and the woods, which are cared for as a natural extension of Henry Middleton's design. Ponds and pools like the ones at Middleton Place were traditional decorative elements of European landscape design. Middleton Americanized his ponds by utilizing them as reservoirs for the rice fields to which they were joined by underground pipes.

We walked around the narrow south side of the pool, keeping a sheep-cropped greensward to our right and following the well-barbered path to a heap of bricks at the site of what had been the main dwelling house. Built before Henry Middleton took possession of the place, the house was burned in February 1865 by soldiers attached to General William T. Sherman's army. The gardens, which the Middletons inwardly identified with their self-conceptions and political ideals, were inexplicably spared.

Situated to catch the summer breezes and afford breathtaking views, the house had looked down a terraced slope to the oncoming river that rolled out like a carpet, east to west, and deposited visitors at the foot of the earthen stairs. To the south of the house was a mill pond that released water to turn a wheel that moved two heavy millstones in a small brick building adjacent to the boat landing. To the north were rice fields, which would have been flooded or dry according to the needs of the growing crop and depending, too, on what the planter wanted to do with the fields between harvest time and planting. Flooded in winter, they would attract migra-

tory ducks who would feast on the rice refuse and make welcome additions to the dinner table. Today the fields are kept permanently submerged, giving the impression that the light that plays on the gleaming surface is a foundation element of the lands.

From the ruins of the house, we walked to a camellia garden overlooking the terraces and two artificial ponds in the shape of butterfly wings, one bordering the south bank of the rice fields, the other abutting the Rice Mill Pond. The four *Camellia japonicas* originally planted in this parterre were special: They were given to the Middleton family by French botanist André Michaux, who may have supervised their planting, in 1786. Three of the four glossy-leafed evergreens have since died and the 8-foot plant that survives is ailing and reduced to one-third its former size. Fraser cannot find this distinctive camellia in any plant catalog, so to produce an heir true to the parent he is propagating it through a process called air-layering. Elated at the apparent success of the experiment, the soft-spoken gardener explained how he did it. He cut away a ring of bark from a healthy branch and scraped off the green tissue or cambium layer, exposing the wood. The wound was swaddled with moistened Spanish moss, and wrapped tightly in plastic, to inhibit evaporation and to prevent the rain from getting in. Fraser's first trials with this method met with failure. A colleague suggested that pesticides might be interfering with propagation, so he ordered spraying stopped and tried again. After about three months a hard mesh of roots and moss filled the plastic sack, and the branch was ready for cutting. Michaux's camellia would live on.

So more than two hundred years after visiting Middleton Place, André Michaux has

Near the Azalea Pool
Middleton Place

been instrumental in the career of an African-American horticulturist who in turn has rescued a piece of the botanist's legacy. Following a plant-collecting expedition to the Near East, which took him from the Indian Ocean to the Caspian Sea, Michaux had come to America in search of plants for French gardens and arboreta. With his teenage son François, he established a "French Garden" at Goose Creek, 10 miles from Charleston, where he prepared specimens and seeds for shipment. The American plants he sent to his homeland include the yellow-flowered star anise; the fragrant loblolly bay; the small silver-bell tree, with its bell-shaped, white flowers; the sword-leafed Spanish bayonet, also called Spanish dagger, a yucca plant of the agave family; and the delectable yellow jasmine, with its sweet-smelling, funnel-shaped flowers. These specimens, along with many others he had collected in his travels, would be lost in the havoc of the French Revolution.

The Old World plants Michaux introduced to America through the port of Charleston fared better than the New World plants he sent abroad. The mimosa, or silk tree, with its spikes of small flowers; the fan-leafed ginkgo, or maidenhair tree, whose foul-smelling seed encases an edible kernel; the Chinese tallow or candleberry tree, native to the Pacific Islands, whose fruit was used in candlemaking; the ornamental crepe myrtle, so named for its crinkled, crepelike pinkish flowers; and the beloved camellia, with its waxy, many-petaled blossoms, have become so commonplace in Southern yards and gardens, and in the woods and untended places which they have colonized, they are popularly mistaken for natives. But what we have come to regard as quintessentially Southern plants, which have spread to cooler latitudes since

being introduced in Charleston, are really sojourners from Asia who followed their discoverer to America.

Michaux left Charleston for good in 1792. (He died, ten years later, while on a plant-collecting trip in Madagascar, home of the rice seed that had transformed the low country a century earlier.) The long growing season, the great variety of native flora, a community of like-minded, knowledgeable plant lovers, and a strong tradition of gardening, continued to make Charleston a haven for botanists as well as for students of other branches of nature and human nature.

Business and pleasure merged in the worlds of planters who also gardened. They competed with one another for the privilege of playing host to visiting plant collectors, nurserymen, foresters, and florists. They experimented on their own, improving the seeds, composts, and fertilizers vital to their agricultural fortunes. They introduced and developed new plant varieties. Champneys Pink Cluster, the first rose to be hybridized in America, came into being around 1811 when rice planter John Champneys crossed an Old Blush rose and a white musk variety. Joel Poinsett, a Huguenot descendant who gardened at both his plantation and his house in town, gave his friends specimens of an unusual plant he had found while serving as United States Ambassador to Mexico. Named for him, the poinsettia, with its tapering red leaves disguised as flower petals, has become a favorite American Christmas ornamental.

The popular gardenia was also named for a resident of Charleston. Scottish-born Alexander Garden emigrated to Charleston in 1752 at age 24 and practiced medicine there for thirty years. His true interests were botanical, and he corresponded with Swedish bota-

nist Carolus Linnaeus, founder of the system of binomial nomenclature that is the basis for modern taxonomy. Linnaeus mused on the cape jasmine, erroneously thought to be native to the Cape of Good Hope, and honored his friend by calling its genus *Gardenia.*

Charleston's Lutheran minister, John Bachman, an émigré from New York State, stocked his garden with woodbine, dogwood, and Cherokee roses he had dug up in the woods. Known to bird lovers for his friendship with John Audubon—they met when Audubon came to town to sell subscriptions to his great work in progress, *The Birds of America*—Bachman cared more about companionable plants and the relationships of plants to animals than he did about questions of scale and detail which were central to the philosophy of the Charleston garden. Audubon moved into Bachman's house and commissioned the minister's sister-in-law, Maria Martin, to paint the botanical backgrounds for at least twenty of his bird plates. No one named a plant for Bachman, but Audubon did name a small songbird for him, the elusive, yellow-cheeked, black-throated Bachman's warbler, a rare bird in their time and today probably extinct.

The first Henry Middleton approached landscape design as a problem in plane geometry. He expressed himself in points, lines, and shapes, particularly the triangle. He combined his gardens with "borrowed vistas" to achieve a private conception, a figure in his mind's eye. Grandson Henry, a contemporary of Champneys and Poinsett, made his mark on the gardens by introducing color. Just returned from England, he placed an order with an English nursery for more than two hundred varieties of flower seeds, bulbs, shrubs, greenhouse plants, herbs, and vegetables.

From the list, we can see that young Henry had a taste for garlic, onions, and leafy greens.

If these delicacies suggest a certain democratic flavor, so do the Old World flowers he asked for which were reared in the gardens, borders, flowerbeds and boxes of the new middle classes. Many flowers the English nurture have come to the island nation from other parts of the globe. The spoils of conquest and curiosity, these varieties had been turning every oceangoing ship into a botanical Noah's ark since an Italian sailor, Giovanni Caboto, a.k.a. John Cabot, explored the coast of North America for the English crown in 1497. More than three hundred years later, Henry Middleton was facilitating the exchange of plants, not so much by introducing new varieties into America, for many of them had long ago made themselves at home here, but by displaying and disseminating them.

The names of the China aster, Moldavian balm (of the mint family, with dense spikes of blue or white flowers), Chilean bellflower, and Marvel of Peru, which we know today by its petalless, long-tubed flowers as the four-o'clock, indicate places that Europeans might have first spied them. The French marigold Middleton ordered was indigenous to Mexico. The annual mignonette, from the familiar latitude of Egypt, would give his gardens a splash of bright color, while the larkspurs, of the genus *Delphinium* and the buttercup family, from the cooler latitudes of Switzerland and Siberia, would show a more somber blue.

The Levant, which took in all the countries bordering the eastern Mediterranean in the horseshoe between Greece and Egypt, was the source of bulbs for Dutch and Roman hyacinth, and for several varieties of narcissus. The autumn crocus on Middleton's list had been grown in England for as long as people could remember. He called for bulbs for six types of amaryllis, including the vittata from Barbados and the belladonna lily from the Cape of Good Hope.

If a right triangle were superimposed on the gardens and grounds of Middleton Place when the house was yet standing, one side would form the main east-west axis, a line extending from the gate at the road to the back steps of the house, through the central hall and the entranceway to the front door, continuing out and descending the bluff through the points of the terraces. The terraces bend with the river. Crafted between 1741 and 1751 by the elder Henry Middleton's slaves applying their earthmoving skills in the rice crop's off-season to a half-mile stretch of river bluff, the raised, flat mounds of earth, symmetrically stacked one above the other, evoke the hillsides of the Mediterranean. These terraces had no agricultural function, however. They did not create level ground for holding olive trees. Looked down upon from the house, looked up at from the river, they told you that man had perfected nature by turning a humble slope into a formal vista. Philosophically, they were closer to Classical Rome than to contemporary Italy.

The Butterfly Lakes between the terraces and the boat landing are attempts to imitate nature that do not seem compatible with Middleton's mathematical scheme. In fact, they do not appear on early plats and drawings, and they are not alluded to in any written record from the eighteenth century. They are consistent with a romantic notion of gardens and an empathy with nature that more likely belonged to the first Henry's great-grandson, the second Henry's son, Williams, who is credited with introducing the first azaleas to the gardens sometime after 1846. The Butterfly Lakes may have been added during his tenure. They are mentioned briefly in an account of the great earthquake of 1886: "Fissures appeared on the surface [of the ground], trees and landscape convoluted, and the lakes at the bottom of the terraces were sucked dry." Alicia Hopton Middleton, in a delightfully outrageous memoir, recalls that "curious Turkish water cattle grazed and revelled" in what must have been the Rice Mill Pond or one of the Butterfly Lakes. The animals stood so deep "that only their noses were visible on the surface." She claims "they were carried off by the Federal troops at the end of the war," and that she "last saw them on exhibition in Central Park in New York."

To conceive of Henry Middleton's geometric scheme, it might help to be seated on a horse, to have "the sovereignty of vision" that he alone had as he surveyed his triangle from a height. The base of the triangle runs north-south through the Reflection Pool, forming a right angle with the main axis at a point about halfway along the line between the gate and the ruins of the dwelling. The hypotenuse of this triangle roughly parallels the rice fields. Running from the center of the terraces at the top of the bluff to the north side of the Reflection Pool, this line diagonally bisects a formal octagonal garden that was once a bowling green, passing through the heart of a birdbath at the center of the form. The hypotenuse splits the Sundial Garden, making two half-moons of the dial. This line had been obscured by 250 years of growth when Hurricane Hugo opened the view in 1989, and the garden suddenly began speaking.

The area between the hypotenuse, or Middleton's diagonal axis, and the two other axes contains a series of small, intimate retreats known as secret gardens where, hedged off from the uninvited, family and guests could enjoy privacy in a parklike atmosphere. Safely inside the triangle, Arthur Middleton, who came between the two Henrys, rests in his tomb just north of the camellia allées. A giant crepe myrtle, another gift from Michaux, still flowers between the axes of the triangle. You can take this triangle, Merrill Robling explained to me, and flip it along Middleton's main axis, using the point at the terraces as a fulcrum, and the visual lineup of elements—trees, parterres, work buildings—would support Middleton's concept of order. I tried flipping the triangle north to south along the main axis. The new hypotenuse, I found, would skirt the slave cemetery and run through the area set up today as a fowl house and hog crawl, before crossing a stream that feeds the Rice Mill Pond. The location of the main slave quarters, which housed the field hands, house servants, cooks, mechanics, gardeners, cattle and sheep minders, carpenters, coopers, tanners, potters, and basketmakers, has not been positively identified in the modern restoration of Middleton Place—a sin of omission shared by other plantations and gardens that have not figured out how to represent slavery. But if current interpretation is correct, and the cabins occupied the area now used as a stable yard, the quarters would have been diagonally bisected by this imaginary line.

A study in the esthetics of symmetry, Henry Middleton's gardens survived two serious challenges before 1800. The first came during the Revolutionary War when British troops trashed the grounds and broke the heads off the marble statues that had been too large to bury or hide. The wood nymph who sits between the sundial and the Azalea Pool, her back turned to the path leading from the formal gardens, is a lonesome reminder of the stone tribe.

The second challenge was theoretical. Thirty years before reaching Charleston, a reaction began building in England against the geometric patterns of Continental gardens like the ones designed by André LeNôtre in Versailles, which had inspired Henry Middleton. Landscape design critic Lancelot Brown, nicknamed "Capability," declared that symmetrical, high-maintenance gardens were obsolete. The garden that was correct for the time should imitate the forms and flow of nature. No longer should we think of nature as an adversary to be held at bay. Nature had been conquered—by the plow, the axe, the gun, and the sailing ship—and now it must be preserved. In the modern garden, the wilderness would make its last stand.

First in England, then in America, gardeners took up their shovels and spades, dug up their parterres, laid low their terraces, demolished the boundaries between the formal and the informal, the planted and the wild. But not Arthur Middleton. He left his father's gardens as they were. It was his era of stewardship, his duty to conserve and increase the family estate and protect its heirlooms. At 34, he had signed the Declaration of Independence; he was not about to ape English fashion, though he knew that in matters of business, religion, and diplomacy, English ideas and institutions had to be acknowledged. But this was the low country of South Carolina, in another land. Forest and the swamp, in alliance with water, were all too ready to reclaim the fields and gardens. The planter's problem was not how to get his crop to grow but how to stop its competitors from growing. Arthur Middleton may have had this in mind, or he may have thought that renovating the gardens was a waste of money and labor. To take no action was, in hindsight, a political act. Whether he consciously intended to perpetuate a work of science and art that reflected man in the right relationship to nature, or was indifferent to symbolic meanings and was simply caring for the estate in his trust, Arthur Middleton held to his father's standard and passed it on to his son.

Of course, the gardens at Middleton Place, like all gardens everywhere, are always changing. Plant growth, reproduction, and death make sure of that. So does the work of gardening. In no two years will the tree line be the same, or the shadows, or the intensity of colors. Blossoms that appear the last week of April one year may show the first of May the next. Because all plants will not be backward or forward in the same season, the coincidence of blooms will vary. Arthur's son Henry brought change to the gardens by introducing hundreds of new plants. His son Williams, who loved azaleas, introduced the tea-olive to the Octagonal Garden and planted the line of magnolia trees on the long east side of the Reflection Pool. He preferred working in the less formal areas, across boundaries, with commonplace materials. When Williams inherited the gardens in 1846, Charleston was receiving a great many Northerners who wanted to see how people lived in the South. Middleton Place belonged to the class of "show" plantations where, as Frederick Law Olmsted, indefatigable traveler and soon-to-be architect of New York City's Central Park, reported in the words of one local, "they have everything fixed up nice."

While they kept up their gardens, low-country planters allowed their money crop "to starve everything else." William Grayson, poet, collector of customs at Charleston, and former

"U.S. Naval Support Base, Somewhere, South Vietnam,"

military exhibit at Patriots Point

Mount Pleasant

owner of a Sea Island cotton plantation, decried the intensification of cotton and rice agriculture. By 1850, plantations had become factories "rearing a crop for foreign markets and little more." Once-numerous fruit orchards had "almost disappeared. Oranges are rare, pomegranates formerly seen everywhere are seldom met with, figs are scarce and small. Few planters have a good peach or strawberry." Even the fish and game had mysteriously declined.

To Grayson, specialization was a matter of life and death, settled on the side of death. The tragedy of specialization, he warned in his 1862 memoir, written from exile in the upcountry, was not simply the passing of a happy, harmonious way of life, but the prospect that planting for the maximum yield would destroy the fabric of society. Strained to produce the most it could year after year, the land would produce progressively less. It would lose its steady, sustainable, low-country character. When prices for rice and cotton fell, as they must, the land would hardly be worth handing down to one's children, or waiting around to inherit.

How could planters be so blind to what they were doing, he wondered? It was objectionable for them to buy their pianos and pineapples from Northern merchants, but unforgivable to buy butter churned in New York, corn grown in Pennsylvania, cider pressed in Vermont, and hogs raised in Tennessee, any and all of which could be produced at home. Even oysters from Northern bays found a market in Charleston, though low-country waters teemed with shellfish.

Grayson longed for the golden age of mixed farming and conservation of natural resources, which he identified with his grandfather's generation. In *The Hireling and*

the Slave, a rejoinder in verse to *Uncle Tom's Cabin*, Grayson defended slavery as the right relation of capital to labor. Now he urged a return to the right relation to the land. Or rather, knowing that it was not to be, and that he was nearing the end of his life, he lamented the missed chance to save Southern prosperity without resorting to a war that, from his perspective, was already lost.

Reform along very different lines was proposed by a Virginia planter with close connections to Charleston. Despairing of achieving agricultural independence through programs of crop rotation and heavy manuring, and obsessed with a Malthusian anxiety that population growth would outstrip food production, Edmund Ruffin proposed what historian Jack Kirby describes as "nothing less than complete reconstruction of the low country"—from the Chickahominy River, in Virginia, to the Savannah, on the South Carolina and Georgia line. Ruffin had conducted a geological survey of South Carolina for Governor James Hammond in 1843, so he knew firsthand the physical nature of the country. Never patient with tinkering, Ruffin was prepared to transform the "half-drowned" tidewater region into another Holland. He would duplicate the Italians' assault on the wetlands of the Po River and eradicate Carolina's "worthless and pestilent swamps." Shallow rivers like the Ashley would be dredged for navigation. Other rivers might be dammed and diverted, to provide relief from flooding and water for irrigation. Canals connecting the rivers would be dug, so that every farmer had a highway to market in a patchquilt landscape threaded by water. Drainage, irrigation, and improved transportation would revive the old Southeast, which was losing business and people to the new Southwest. Banked and

canalled, 3,000 square miles of the coastal South would look like one vast rice plantation. If Grayson wanted to change people, Ruffin wanted to reshape the land.

Land reclamation on this scale would have required untold sums of money and a degree of cooperation at odds with planters' traditions and pride. If they could not agree on furnishing hands to work the roads, how would they ever join forces to reconstruct the environment? Ruffin presented his ideas to friendly, if apathetic, ears in Charleston in 1852. As the decade wore on, Ruffin's infirmities slowed him down, while hatred of the North consumed him. Present at the firing on Fort Sumter, he had himself photographed in the uniform of the South Carolina militia. The war was particularly cruel to him. After a son and a grandson were killed and his prized library was looted by the Yankees, he stuck the muzzle of his musket in his mouth and blew his head off.

Poor drainage had plagued Charleston from the first days. The salt water that wrapped the low-lying peninsula gave some relief from the malarial swamps, but the salt soured wells and compromised hygiene. Privies discharged into shallow canals clogged by kitchen waste and animal carcasses, contaminating the groundwater. It took heavy rain at low tide to clean out the canals, rain that left behind stagnant pools where mosquitoes bred by the millions. Rampant gastrointestinal diseases reflected the state of sanitation and the water supply.

Charleston was simply too flat for the system of drains that vented into the Cooper River. A ditch that ran along today's Calhoun Street fell only 2 ½ inches per 100 feet, compared to a 5- to 10-inch descent in the sewers

Summer flood

Washington and Charlotte Streets

of London. The city surveyor came up with an ingenious solution. He proposed replacing the system of "inclined planes" with a level system that flushed with the tides. The city might overcome its lack of elevation by taking advantage of the difference in the height of the water in the Ashley and Cooper rivers. It had been observed from the wharves, wrote surveyor Charles Parker, that the Ashley River rose and fell with the harbor, "but that the Cooper, being a long and deep river with several considerable tributaries . . . consumed more time to fill and empty," and thus would "maintain flood and ebb to a later hour." He advised digging a channel from river to river and, applying technology from the rice fields to a problem in urban ecology, installing a series of gates which would impound water from one river and send it coursing to the other in "an artificial rush," carrying the city's wastes in the flow.

The idea was never tried, and it remains a fascinating artifact in the records of plans for getting the land "right" with the water. Nowhere else in the South were agriculture and health so dependent on altering the relation of land to water, and only in the river-bordered sugar lands, and then only in the pioneer stage, did cultivators outside the low country have to reshape the environment. A sensitivity to gradations and planes, driven by a wish to make three dimensions out of two, characterized the mentality of low-country gardeners and planters, surveyors and geologists.

Edmund Ruffin is an example of a geologist who was concerned both with the structure of the earth's crust and with fossils. He was primarily interested in identifying deposits of fossilized shells and mining them for fertilizer. For thirty years, he exhorted planters to use calcium-rich limestone or calcareous manures on their lands to improve productivity. Other geologists may have used the fossil record to justify existing social arrangements, but Ruffin stuck to issues involving physical, and not human, nature. Never wavering in his certainty about black inferiority, he nonetheless kept silent in the debate over the creation of the races.

The same cannot be said for his friend, John Bachman. While spokesmen for the new sciences of anthropology, paleontology, and zoology at colleges in Boston and Philadelphia were promoting the theory of polygenesis, or the separate creation of whites and blacks, the Charleston minister took the opposing position that all human beings are descended from a single pair. Bachman's name became synonymous with the theory of monogenesis, or single creation. A Southerner by choice, slave owner, and preacher of the Gospel, Bachman may seem at first to be an unlikely candidate for this mantle. But he never lost his childhood curiosity for the natural world and the habit of systematic observation that took him down the intellectual path traveled by his acquaintance, Charles Darwin. Bachman had met Darwin in England, shortly after the young naturalist returned from his voyage to the Galapagos Islands in 1839. The theory of common descent percolated in their minds for decades before each man committed it to print.

Charleston was hardly a hospitable place for a monogenesist to take a stand. In 1847, Harvard zoologist Louis Agassiz told an adoring audience at Charleston's Philosophical Society that science supports the view of species as static, nonchanging entities. Bachman dissented, and in 1850 he quietly published his rebuttal, *The Unity of the Human Species*. The *Charleston Medical Journal* used the death of geologist Samuel George Morton, past presi-dent of Philadelphia's Academy of Natural Sciences, as an occasion to take a slap at Bachman's views and to affirm the social and scientific orthodoxy of the times. "We of the South should consider him as our benefactor," Morton was eulogized, "for aiding materially in giving to the negro his true position as an inferior race."

The scientific question of the unity of man and the political question of slavery, wrote Jay Shuler, Bachman's discerning biographer, "both moved toward resolution as the 1850s drew to a close." Darwin published *On the Origin of Species* in 1859. (At one point he quoted from Bachman's review of Agassiz's "Sketch of the Natural Provinces of the Animal World" to support his argument for the process of natural selection.) Darwin, like Bachman, argued that races are not found in nature, but must be accounted for in history. Both men disputed the age of the earth calculated by church authorities as too young to sustain the evolution of complex life. They debunked the idea that man occupies a unique position in creation, and that the white man has a special place in the hierarchy of races. It was the social system, in their view, not random nature, that distributed opportunities for races and individuals to migrate, reproduce, and change.

Yet when the Southern states began seceding from the Union in 1860, the man who would deliver the benediction at South Carolina's secession convention was the same man who upheld the standard for a single creation, while his abolition-minded friends in the North defended the doctrine of human disunity. Somehow, Bachman could avow a biological kinship between whites and blacks, and at the same time approve of slavery. We may be baffled by the apparent contradiction, but he was not. Bachman took the practical position of a person living wholly in his times, not in ours. Whether slaveholders believed, if they thought about it at all, that slavery was ordained by God, decreed by nature, or imposed on them by greedy traders from outside the South, they deemed it "indispensable," in Edmund Ruffin's words, "to the greatest profits" extractable from Southern soils. Slave labor, Ruffin would argue, was the South's way of putting man and land in the right relation.

Combining nineteenth-century science's concern for human differences with empirical evidence from the rice and cotton fields of his state, South Carolina College President Thomas Cooper expressed the popular belief that slavery was justified both by the nature of the soil and the nature of the climate "which incapacitates a white man from laboring in the summer time." Bachman never addressed the climate issue directly, but I can guess how a Bachmanite would reply. He might point out, with plantation scholar Edgar T. Thompson, that climatic theories tend to arise in interracial situations. They tend to support the view that social distinctions are biological in origin and not "the result of history and circumstances." Though weather may certainly distinguish one place from another, a theory that makes agricultural slavery dependent "upon a fixed and static something like climate," outside of human interaction, is a product of the system but not an explanation of it.

A visit to Middleton Place in April 1933, moved Vita Sackville-West, the English poet, to ask:

Stand I indeed in England? Do I dream?
Those broken steps, those grassy terraces,
Those water-meadows, and that ample stream,

Do they indeed but cheat my heart, my eyes,
With their strange likeness to the thing they seem?
—Vita Sackville-West, "Middleton Place, South Carolina"

The gardens were being painstakingly restored by J.J. Pringle Smith, a cousin of Williams Middleton's daughter Elizabeth, who had willed it to him in 1915, and Smith's wife, Heningham. The young couple found the gardens, in Heningham's words, "a wilderness overgrown with tangled honeysuckle, Southern smilax and bramble; yellow jessamine completely covering the great groups of camellia bushes . . . ." Heningham got down on her hands and knees and identified the outlines of the brick pathways by touch. Affirmed by a trip to a Middleton estate in England, the Smiths cut back the jungle, replanted flower beds, reestablished, then artfully concealed, the boundary between formal areas and the natural forest, and opened the gardens to the public for three months every spring. There was no staple crop to subsidize the cost of restoring the grounds, and while Pringle and Heningham threw their backs into the labor, a work force had to be paid. Rich in land but poor in cash, and suffering like almost everyone in rural America from economic depression, the Smiths took a step some of the English cousins were also driven to: They began making plants their business. They started out shipping homegrown azaleas. Soon they were selling commercial supplies of flowers and vegetables.

This was not England, however. Sackville-West would return to the ruined castle of Sissinghurst in Kent and win fame in its gardens, knowing that she had been "tricked" by a sameness that was really "nature's difference" into imagining that Middleton Place was

a part of England. Like the Englishmen who had gone to Carolina before her and "cut their English shapes" in a forest on the banks of a river as "sleepy as Thames," she is overpowered by the New World. The grammar or principles of the gardens may indeed be English, but the vocabulary is distinctly American—not only the indigenous plants and birds with their undomesticated mystery, but naturalized trees and shrubs that grow faster and wilder here, deepened "the secret of the southern day."

Sackville-West paints the exhilarating scene with sure, quick strokes. Sensitive to dangers that lurk below the surface of an alien place, she records details that would have caught the eye of George Orwell. In England, there never "squatted near a pile/of oranges, their morning labour done/That group of negroes idle in the shade." The oranges tell us we are not just in any part of the South, but in the tropical south, an outpost of the Indies. The "negroes" indicate America. Proper Englishmen and women never squat. Well-bred people may take their rest, but they are never idle. Orwell would say the dark-skinned laborers are part of the secret that everyone knows but them. The power to change things is in their hands. What will they do, he would ask, when they wake up from their repose?

"No England!" then, at Middleton Place, but something close, a look, an echoing tone
Such as may cross the voice of distant kin,
Caught briefly, swiftly flown,
Different in resemblance, held within
A heart still mindful of the English way."

Jump-started by an appreciation of "The Ashley River and its Gardens" in *National Geographic Magazine* in May 1926, and benefiting from association with the literary and artistic movement known as the Charleston Renaissance, annual tourist visits to Middleton Place climbed into the thousands. The plantation romance had become white America's "chief social idyll of the past," a picturesque way of life filled with purpose and pleasure. The fact that it ended in bloody war only seemed to enhance its appeal. In the wake of the sensational success of Margaret Mitchell's novel *Gone with the Wind* in 1936, the gardens at Middleton Place became a sanctuary for visitors seeking a living reminder of better times. Pringle and Heningham Smith gardened because, like his Middleton ancestors, they loved plants and felt a duty to family. They found joy in replenishing and transforming their gardens by introducing many native and exotic specimens, including some twenty hairy Chinese chestnut trees. Yet, to worshippers of the past, the altered gardens were a bulwark against change, a symbol of the right to retain one's customs against the forces of Modernism.

The gardens' rise from the ashes of war and the rubble of earthquake and storm was not equaled by the economy. Decades of natural and man-made disasters had returned the low country to an economic frontier. In 1900, the port of Charleston was as full of promise as the day the English first crossed the bar and sounded the channel. South and west of the city, asymmetric truck farms, now the dominant agricultural units, nestled against the ubiquitous marshes. Industrial activity was largely confined to fertilizer factories on the banks of the Ashley that processed phosphates mined in the riverbed.

Hoping to attract investment to Charleston, the city hosted a great fair, the South Carolina and West Indian Exposition, in 1901-02. The fairgrounds covered 250 acres, including most of what is now Hampton Park, with frontage on the Ashley River. Exhibitions housed in alabaster "palaces" showed off the industrial and agricultural potential of the low country. Just as William Hilton had described the province of Carolina as the northernmost outpost of the West Indies, promoters of tourism in the twentieth century emphasized the low country's island heritage, including its servant population of African-cultured people.

By the time of the exposition, the former agricultural landscape had been greatly modified. Rice production was limited to a few old tracts. (Hurricanes in 1911 and 1916 would drive the last nails into the industry's coffin.) Sea Island cotton was scarcely produced and while large pieces of the old Sea Island and mainland plantations were yet intact, they were bordered on the land side by small farms and cabins, by open spaces forever sprouting weeds and pine trees, and by pine forests in various stages of succession. With few exceptions, white people retained control of the riverbanks and seashore. Mild winters and fine sea breezes made the Sea Islands attractive to wealthy Northerners who leased or bought plantations and kept them for hunting and partying. Timber companies cut down the forests using technology to overcome environmental constraints. My neighbor York McGinnis recalled the tram railways laid over bog and thicket and removed once the harvestable logs were brought out. Before he settled into farming and raising a family, Mr. York lived the migratory life of a turpentine worker, chipping boxes in longleaf pine trees—the method of extracting pine sap for making turpentine and pitch—and moving from camp to camp as the forests were exhausted.

Another neighbor of mine, old Dick Stoll, supplied us for years with corn, sweet potatoes, and melons from his fields, grapes from his arbors, and peaches from his trees. The caretaker of a duck pond used on weekends by its upcountry owner, Stoll was hired to maintain the banks and floodgates, move water on and off the pond, and nurture the widgeon grass that ducks like to eat. Mr. Stoll's father, who was of German descent, took advantage of the frontierlike conditions and acquired land in the post-plantation era. His mother worked in an oyster-shucking factory.

Besides farming and keeping up a market garden, Dick Stoll worked on dredge boats, raised bees, and was constantly inventing things to deal with environmental challenges. He devised a trap to catch the Mediterranean fruit fly, and rumor has it that he was secretly wealthy. Mr. Stoll was always trapping or shooting something, whether for food or to eliminate birds and animals who ate his corn and grapes—varmints, he called them. He was kind to me, however, and he was fond of talking.

One day, we were discussing rice operations on the Santee that he had observed as a boy. He told me that a great white civilization had come by sea to the low country many hundreds of years ago, cleared the swamps and built the rice impoundments. Then they got back on their ships and disappeared. Englishmen and Africans arrived later and, finding the country deserted, they appropriated the handiwork of the lost civilization and planted rice. So his father told him. It was inconceivable to Mr. Stoll, who had lived and worked around black people all his life, that slaves wielding shovels in ankle-deep mud could have moved that much earth.

A different account of the origin of the rice banks was given by an anonymous exslave, whose landlord wanted to kick him off

Construction of Charleston Harbor Hilton Resort
Patriots Point

the plantation when he grew too old to work. "De strength of dese arms and dese legs and of dis old back is in your rice bank," the black man chided his boss. He had given his life to the earthworks and was entitled to consideration. Not that building and repairing the rice banks were activities he would have chosen. Digging in mud was hated work. After the Civil War, free men and women on Sea Island cotton plantations balked at having to dig marsh mud and to spread it in the fields. Elixirs composed of mud and manure gave way to store-bought fertilizers. On rice plantations, there was conflict between employers wanting their contract hands to do battle with the environment in gangs, and workers insisting on preserving their tasks.

If it were possible to ask a slave what he or she was doing in life, it is absurd to think the answer would be "growing as much rice as possible for the master." More likely answers are: getting enough to eat and drink; finding intimacy and elbow room in tight quarters; trying to stay healthy and avoid overworking; caring for spouses, children, other relatives, and friends; having a good time and staying out of trouble. The problem of representing slavery to visitors at Middleton Place, and on other low-country plantations, is complex and controversial. First, there is the overarching difficulty that the slave's routine was tedious and nasty. Second, though the gardens would not exist without the labor and other inputs of the black people who once lived at Middleton Place, the grounds preserve the architectural and esthetic choices of the masters and their hired gardeners, from the first Henry Middleton through the board and director of Middleton Place Foundation, which runs the gardens today on a not-for-profit basis, and horticulturist Sidney Fraser. These people

have made splendid choices through the ages, but they are not the choices that tell us how the rice hands made use of space for their own purposes. Slaves built the banks and worked the crops. They planted the formal gardens and gardens of their own. They laid the bricks and sawed the lumber for their master's house and put up the barns and an array of outbuildings, yet their own dwellings have left no visible traces. They, too, peered across the river. But did they see what the planter saw?

A window to the world of the slaves has been opened by the pioneering work of plantation archaeologists. Prodded by the Civil Rights Movement to take the African-American past seriously, the University of South Carolina's Leland Ferguson began excavating colonial black sites in the old rice lands along the upper reaches of the Cooper River. On Middleburg Plantation, northeast of Middleton Place, the clay walls of the early houses have long since returned to earth, but the heart-pine posts that reinforced the walls have left dark stains in the sandy yellow subsoil. Such evidence throws light on the orientation of the cabins; their size and the arrangement of rooms; the division of space into cooking, eating, and sleeping areas; the layout of the yard and common areas between houses; the distance from house to house.

Trash heaps just outside the door yield telling treasures such as charred pieces of animal bone, glass fragments, buttons, broken tools, and pieces of pottery. The humble clay pot played a crucial part in Ferguson's thinking. He recalled a find of hand-built, unglazed pottery at Williamsburg, Virginia, that had been labeled "Colono-Indian ware," referring to its supposed Indian artisans. Discoveries of similar pottery in South Carolina and the sheer quantity of it forced him to reconsider.

Ferguson wondered whether clay pots formerly attributed to Indians might have been made instead by African Americans. He was encouraged by a letter from a colleague in Ghana comparing West African pottery to Colono-Indian ware. Driving by the basket stands in Mt. Pleasant, across the Cooper River from Charleston, it occurred to him that just as basketry survived the trauma of enslavement, pottery might have, too.

Ferguson's team of investigators set about mapping the slave quarters at Middleburg and neighboring plantations. The truly radical aspect of this work is how it quietly deconstructs the idea of the plantation. By plotting the footpaths and water routes linking the slave settlements and imagining the comings and goings across plantation lines, Ferguson describes an exogamous black society meandering over a territory with a shape all its own. While their white masters tended to marry within a small circle of property owners that included cousins, black bondsmen and women cast a wider net and sought out mates beyond their immediate social group.

The new picture does not refute the notion of the plantation as the region's characteristic institution as much as it indicates that other patterns of meaning were operating as well. While the planter's ideal landscape confirms his mastery over land and men, and in essence his detachment from them, the scenery taken in by the slaves is a guide to the location of people who validate their existence and provide a congenial thicket in which they might lose themselves. Advertisements for runaway slaves in the eighteenth century typically surmise that the villains have run to their relatives, sometimes taking the master's horse or skiff. Slave hunters might find this information useful, but just as often the advertisement informs us that the runaways have relatives in all directions. Where the planter might "borrow" a vista such as a line of cypress trees across the river to fit a geometric pattern, a slave might perceive a likely place to harbor a canoe. The planter's vision of nature is political and esthetic; the slave's vision is intensely social. In years to come, interpreters of the past at Middleton Place may be able to tell us which elements of the landscape black people found useful and beautiful. Neither the slaves' perspective nor the master's can tell the whole story, however, because plantation culture, which influences how Americans think and act today, was more complicated than a series of separate traditions.

As we drove to Charleston one day along recently four-laned Highway 17, Mr. York pointed to the tall pine forest out the driver's-side window and told me that you used to be able to see out across the cotton fields to the salt marshes and the beach. When cotton farming ceased, many of the old fields were allowed to grow up in pine, though here and there beans and cucumbers were planted, until they too are only a memory. The horticultural forest sweeps east-west with minor interruptions from the shore to cypress swamps, 4 to 6 miles inland, that once were impounded for rice and have long since been reclaimed by nature. Several wetlands in the Francis Marion National Forest have been designated as wilderness areas and will be subject to minimal human disturbance, but for the rest, fast-growing pines planted over previous clearcuts crowd out hardwoods whose growth is further discouraged by poisoning and fire. Hurricane Hugo leveled the forest in 1989, creating a landscape of broken sticks above which those pesky deciduous trees dare to peek.

Before there was a bridge over the Cooper River, Mr. York occasionally ferried a wagonload of produce, firewood, or moonshine into Charleston. A bridge was completed in 1929, a few years after the paving of the two-lane coastal highway. The roadbed had been laid with truckloads of oyster shells, recycled from rings of shell refuse left by the coastal Indians over a millennium. Like artificial mounds in plantation gardens, which provided heights to enjoy the views, the shell rings were perches for looking out over the flat marsh islands. And like similar structures in Mesoamerica, they may have enabled native people to track the calendar year according to the bearing of the rising sun.

Recently, Highway 17 was designated as the corridor for a new interstate, I-73, which is slated to connect Detroit and Charleston. Drawn on paper in contempt of topography and human geography, I-73 is the latest version of the centuries-old fantasy to find a passage to the Orient that would funnel the wealth of the hinterland through the port of Charleston. I-73 would put a hundred million Americans and Canadians within a day's drive of the low country. With dollar signs spinning in their eye sockets, promoters in Ohio and West Virginia declaim with religious fervor that I-73 would lift their region "out of the mud." Its impact in the low country would be to wipe several towns and settlements hemmed in by wetlands and forests off the face of the earth. The basketmakers of Mt. Pleasant are certain to be affected.

For as long as men and women of African descent have lived in Carolina, they have made baskets out of a marsh grass called bulrush, and in recent times from sweetgrass, a finer grass found where the marsh meets high ground. Whether made under coercion or by free choice, baskets in the slavery era always held more than rice or corn, laundry, fruit, or flowers. In shape and technique, the bulrush basket carried forward African ways that were modified in the low country under the watchful gaze of people from Europe whose traditions and sensibilities were being modified by the same environment.

Originally employed in great numbers on rice plantations, baskets are made today by the grand- and great-grandchildren of the rice hands for show and for sale. Some basketmakers sell their wares at the market in Charleston. But more sell their work at some sixty basket stands along a 12-mile stretch of Highway 17, just above Mt. Pleasant. The spread of residential and commercial development has been dislodging the stands and pushing them up the road. Meanwhile, construction of homes and resorts in the sweetgrass zone has seriously depleted supplies of the grass and closed off access to the remainder.

One consequence of the sweetgrass shortage has been the return to bulrush, and the production of larger, African-looking forms. Basketmakers take inspiration from books and magazines; visits to museums, craft shows, and Wal-Mart, and from trips to Africa itself. As basketmakers on both sides of the Atlantic respond to similar pressures and opportunities, their work undergoes a similar transformation. What art historian John Vlach has said about the low-country basket is true as well for its African kin: "A craft that began with functional intentions has become an art medium with primarily aesthetic motivation."

I-73 would remove the basket stands altogether. Poof! Goodbye! It would be ironic if, at the moment that low-country basketry is achieving artistic recognition, when the basket makers feel free and confident enough to celebrate its African origins, an earth-moving project in high-speed transportation cuts people off from their past. In this sense, I-73 would create greater distances than it would span.

An urban planner might say it's time people left the road and adopted a new strategy for selling their baskets. Even prior to the specter of the interstate, there was talk about herding the basketmakers under the roof of a single all-weather market. The idea won little support from the basketmakers. Used to the free enterprise atmosphere of the road with all its noise and dust, and days when it is too wet or too cold to sit outside, they see the one-stop market as a threat to their autonomy. They like being their own proprietors. They fear losing the liberty to set their own hours, to spread out or tuck in their business according to who may be working with them or learning at their knees, to socialize with family and friends, to customize their weather-tested stands to show their baskets in a manner they deem appropriate. They also prize their artistic independence. Every weaver has her own style, her own favored forms, and her own signature, revealed in her stitching. Baskets made by one person are not interchangeable, in their eyes, with baskets made by another.

Perhaps this resilient legacy would find a way to adapt to the new situation. After all, the lesson of commercial penetration by Northerners in the low country, and by Europeans in Africa, is that contact with foreign influences does not necessarily pollute or kill off native arts and crafts but can give fresh impetus to expressive traditions. Artists and consumers are energized by contact. But contact is not what this interstate would bring. Just as basketmaking expanded with the upgrading of Highway 17, with its welcome shoulders and stream of travelers at leisure to pull off the road, so it would contract with the consuming of the ribbon of high

ground called Mt. Pleasant by the interstate landscape and the hermetic sealing off of potential buyers in their speeding automobiles.

A year before he died, Mr. York sold his last mule, Henry. I was in the yard when a white man drove up to the stable with a trailer hitched to a late 1970s Ford Ranchero, one of those short-lived experiments that combined the cab of a sedan with the hull of a pickup. Mr. York held his hat over his heart as the man loaded up the mule and drove away. He didn't like to see the mule standing in its stall all day and, having cut back his gardening and having outlived the people he used to ride out to visit, he decided to let the mule go. The buyer had no use for the wagon and left it to fall apart where it was unless some antique dealer got a hold of it first.

Like most people, Mr. York wanted to get where he was going without delay. He kept a mule after mules fell out of fashion not because he liked the slow pace and the rhythmic clickety-clack, but because he lived within sight of his limits. He had respect for the carrying capacity of the land, and for his own strength as well. Now, his plowing days done, no more to take, in Thomas Hardy's words, that "slow, silent walk" through his rows, Mr. York worked his last crop with a hoe. He planned to cut back on corn since he no longer had a mule to feed, but to extend his watermelon patch and let the vines take over the deserted rows.

It was early April and the gnats were thick. Mr. York built a small fire upwind of the garden. Aromatic smoke from dry cedar limbs and from the prunings of an old pear tree drenched us and gave relief. The pear was an unusual variety brought here from Texas at a time when the Appalachian Mountains to the west were still more difficult to cross than the ocean to the east.

Two full-bodied walnut trees, immigrants from other parts who had grown old on this land, provided shade until noon. Mr. York knew better than to try to work in full sun. Before quitting for the afternoon, he took a handkerchief out of his pocket and, bowing carefully from the waist, dusted off the colorful empty seed packets impaled on stakes at the head of each row.

The garden was not so large, and his memory not so poor, that he needed to be reminded of what was planted where. Besides, the plants were up, and he knew them as well as he knew his children. The green peas were bearing, and the spinach had already appeared on his table. He was waiting on a can of tar to coat his corn seed and frustrate the birds. He might throw a little soda to the corn when it got up and needed a boost, but that was all he was going to do. I promised to help him keep down the weeds and grass. He sought help from other sources too.

Staking out the seed packets was something Mr. York had begun doing when photographs of the happy, mature plants and their marvelous fruit started appearing on the labels. "Does that bring you luck?" I asked. "No, not luck exactly," he said, "it brings power," like the pulse surging in the veins in his forearms as he clenched his fists for emphasis. This man who would call up the wind with a song was petitioning nature with pretty effigies of Clemson Spineless okra and cane-sweet butter beans. "They're like fertilizer," I ventured. "No, not fertilizer exactly," he corrected me, "more like words." The power of knowing the words that make things grow was given to man by the Creator, he went on, but taken back because man grew too prideful, leaving us with the five powers we inherit at birth. "Don't you know," he laughed, "a picture is worth a hundred words?"

Parking lot, Bedon's Alley
and Elliott Streets

Author's note

Readers who would like to consult the books and articles that have taught me most of what I know about the mutually transforming relationship between environment and human culture in the low country should start with William Hilton's classic chronicle of discovery in *Narratives of Early Carolina 1650–1708* (edited by Alexander S. Salley, Jr., New York: Barnes & Noble, 1967).

The English project in Carolina during the age of exploration is explained in its breadth and nuance by D.W. Meinig in his monumental *The Shaping of America: A Geographical Perspective on 500 Years of History*, Volume I, "Atlantic America, 1492–1800" (New Haven: Yale University Press, 1986). The reader should be warned that once begun, this book is not easily put down.

The best introduction to the aboriginal people encountered by the English, and therefore by the French and Spanish, is Charles M. Hudson's *The Southeast Indians* (Knoxville: University of Tennessee Press, 1976). In "Why the Southeastern Indians Slaughtered Deer," an essay that appears in *Indians, Animals, and the Fur Trade: A Critique of Keepers of the Game*, edited by Shepard Krech II (Athens: University of Georgia Press, 1981), Hudson interprets the Indians' apparently self-defeating ecological behavior in the context of lethal, unremitting pressures applied by land-hungry Europeans. The African role in turning the former Indian realms from subsistence to commercial agriculture is the subject of Peter H. Wood's pathbreaking work on South Carolina's Colonial history, *Black Majority: Negroes in Colonial South Carolina from 1670 through the Stono Rebellion* (New York: Alfred A. Knopf, 1976). Daniel C. Littlefield's *Rice and Slaves: Ethnicity and the Slave Trade in Colonial South Carolina* (Baton Rouge: Louisiana State University Press,

1981) builds on Wood's suggestion that Africans furnished knowledge as well as labor to the tasks of settling Carolina and adjusting the land and water to the requirements of rice production. Important contributions to the history of the low-country agricultural landscape include James M. Clifton's *Life and Labor on Argyle Island: Letters and Documents of a Savannah River Rice Plantation, 1833–1867* (Savannah: The Beehive Press, 1978), Charles Joyner's *Down by the Riverside: A South Carolina Slave Community* (Urbana: University of Illinois Press, 1984), Peter A. Colclanis's *The Shadow of a Dream: Economic Life and Death in the South Carolina Low Country, 1670–1920* (New York: Oxford University Press, 1989), Joyce E. Chaplin's *An Anxious Pursuit: Agricultural Innovation and Modernity in the Lower South, 1730–1815* (Chapel Hill: The University of North Carolina Press, 1993) and Judith A. Carney's "Landscapes Of Technology Transfer: Rice Cultivation and African Continuities" *Technology and Culture*, 37:1 (January, 1996).

Perhaps the finest work on the never-ending negotiation between culture and nature I have ever read is Mart A. Stewart's *"What Nature Suffers to Groe": Life, Labor, and Landscape on the Georgia Coast, 1680–1920* (Athens: University of Georgia Press, 1996). Set in coastal Georgia, much of this study of agricultural and forest labor and their relation to natural energy flows applies intact to the rice and Sea Island cotton zones of Carolina. Jack Temple Kirby's *Poquosin: A Study of Rural Landscape and Society* (Chapel Hill: The University of North Carolina Press, 1995) probes the rural landscape of tidewater Virginia and North Carolina and is a prudent model for thinking about the modification of South Carolina's swamp and river country. Leland Ferguson's *Uncommon Ground: Archeology and Early African*

America, 1650–1800 (Washington, D.C.: Smithsonian Institution Press, 1992) is an archeological thriller that emphasizes the role of the environment in providing conditions and materials for the unique adaptation made by the first African Americans to the Carolina tidal region that resulted in the invention of a lasting culture.

In an impeccably researched, deeply felt essay, "'Still Mindful of the English Way': 250 Years of Middleton Place on the Ashley," which appeared in *South Carolina Historical Magazine*, 92:3 (January, 1991), Elise Pinckney puts us in touch with the warm-blooded people who for more than 200 years have collaborated with nature to create and maintain the magnificent gardens at Middleton Place. James R. Cothran's circuit of Charleston's private gardens, *Gardens of Historic Charleston* (Columbia: University of South Carolina Press, 1995) breathes new life into an old genre of garden tour books. With the aid of superb photographs, he shows how Charleston's urban gardeners have produced gardens of great dignity and pathos.

Henry Savage, who devoted his life to implanting nature into the writing of history, wrote *André and François Andre Michaux* (Charlottesville: University of Virginia Press, 1986), the indispensable biography of the French plant collectors and breeders who turned Charleston into a major hub in the worldwide exchange of trees and flowering shrubs. Jay Shuler's *Had I the Wings: The Friendship of Bachman and Audubon* (Athens: University of Georgia Press, 1995), a stunning account of Charleston's leading nineteenth-century natural scientist, John Bachman, and Bachman's friend, Jean Audubon, is a book that grows in importance as destruction of low-country forests and wetlands moves into high

gear. Atlanta-based photographer John McWilliams, who moors his hand-built sailboat in a creek in front of his cabin near the Santee River, has documented the wounded landscape in *Land of Deepest Shade* (New York: Aperture Foundation in Association with the High Museum of Art, Atlanta, 1989). Dale Rosengarten's soon-to-be-published *Social Origins of the African-American Lowcountry Basket* is a history of the constant, intimate dialogue that the low country's traditional cultivators and their children have carried on with nature.

Even as I try to conclude this note, the titles of other books that clarify the history and plight of the low-country environment leap to mind. The late Patricia Jones-Jackson's *When Roots Die: Endangered Traditions on the Sea Islands* (Athens: University of Georgia Press, 1987), is a deftly analyzed collection of Sea Island tales and prayers whose context and opportunities for presentation are disappearing in the wake of resort development and white cultural imperialism. Wendell Berry's *The Unsettling of America* (San Francisco: Sierra Club Books, 1977) may be about the interface of culture and agriculture in the American uplands, but the crisis he so eloquently lays bare—of the practice of scorning the carrying capacity of the soil, of extracting maximum yields instead of sustainable harvests, and of gleaning the most profit and comfort with the least expenditure of human energy—gets at the heart of the low country's predicament. It is always instructive to see how someone who came before us made a heroic adjustment to the environment. I recommend reading Elizabeth Allston Pringle's *A Woman Rice Planter,* (Columbia: University of South Carolina Press, 1992) for its artistic self-portrayal of a low-country white woman trying to reestablish her relationship to the land, and to the freed men and

women who were once inseparable from the land, during the troubled time that historian Bertram Wyatt-Brown has called "the purgatory of post-Civil War economic decline." An upbeat companion to these books about loss is Jim Nollman's *Why We Garden* (New York: Henry Holt and Company, 1994), a meditation on participating with nature and nourishing the impulses we all come with to learn how to live within a place.

Vincent Scully in "Architecture: The Natural and the Manmade" and John Dixon Hunt in "The Garden as Cultural Object" find the urge to reshape the earth intrinsic to fundamental human activities such as gardening, agriculture, art, and spiritual seeking. Their thoughtful essays appear in *Denatured Visions: Landscape and Culture in the 20th Century*, a book published by the Museum of Modern Art (1991) and edited by Stuart Wrede and William Howard Adams.

Charleston

1

Magdalena Abakanowicz

2

Herb Parker

3

Patrick Dougherty

4

**Philip Simmons and
Pearl Fryar**

5

Martha Jackson-Jarvis

6

Mary Lucier

7

Esther Mahlangu

8

Charles Simonds

Magdalena Abakanowicz

Hand-like Trees

Battery walkway at East Battery Street
and Murray Boulevard

For her part in "Human/Nature," Magdalena Abakanowicz brought to Charleston five massive bronze sculptures, each more than 12 feet tall and weighing more than 2,000 pounds, and arranged them on an elevated, curving walkway at the tip of the peninsula where the Ashley and Cooper rivers meet to form a great estuary. Part of a series called *Hand-like Trees* that the artist has been creating since 1992, the sculptures stood out against the expanse of sky and water, exploring the relationship between human and natural forms in the monumental and expressive terms that have made her an artist of international distinction.

Born into an aristocratic family in Falenty, Poland, in 1930, Abakanowicz grew up on an estate about 125 miles east of Warsaw. From an early age, her life was shaped by an attachment to nature, but also by tragedy. "I had no companions of my own age," she reminisced in an autobiographical essay years later. "I had to fill the enormously long and empty days alone, minutely exploring everything in the environment. Learning about all that was alive—watching, touching, and discovering—was accomplished in solitude. Time was capacious, roomy: Leaves grew slowly and slowly changed their shape and color. Everything was immensely important. All was at one with me."[1]

In 1939, her life changed irrevocably. German tanks rumbled onto her family's lands. "The house exposed us, it ceased to be a shelter. The forest also became alien. I no longer went there to talk to it as before." In 1943, Nazi soldiers attacked her home: "They came at night . . . drunk. They bashed at the door. Mother rushed to open it . . . . She did not make it: They began to fire. A dum-dum bullet tore her right elbow. It severed her arm at the shoulder." The following year, her family fled its estate in advance of the Soviet army, fearful of class antagonisms. Dispossessed, they settled in Warsaw, where Abakanowicz ultimately attended art school, struggling to express her cultural independence in the face of Soviet repression.

Hand-like Trees, from foreground to background:
Desda (1994), *Figura Seconda* (1995), *Figura Prima* (1995), *Balan* (1994), and *Anaka* (1994)
Courtesy Marlborough Gallery, New York

These experiences endowed Abakanowicz's art with both tragedy and stoicism. The hollow, armless and headless figures for which she is best known are reminders of the anonymous victims of war, but they are also embryonic, as if they contained the seeds of their own regeneration. Like many of her other sculptures, the resin-stiffened burlap backs, seated and standing figures were executed in series or cycles; they are commonly exhibited in haunting, semihuman collectives. On one side, these figures are solid; on the other, they are voids, as if disemboweled. They frequently contain rudimentary spines and spikes that resemble broken ribs. They look as if they could be flayed skins or the assembled inmates of a prison camp. Yet they convey some strength in numbers; they suggest a mute but potent force.

Abakanowicz's work first attracted international attention in 1965, when her large mixed-media weavings won the gold medal at the São Paulo Biennale. These were fol-

lowed by the massive fiber *Abakans*, shroudlike hanging textiles, executed in the late 1960s and early 1970s. Always attentive to the possibilities of employing familiar materials in unexpected ways, she was soon using heavy rope, massive wooden spools, and twine in addition to burlap. Her first figures date from the middle of the 1970s; they were shown to great acclaim as the Polish representation at the Venice Biennale in 1980. She began working in bronze in 1985, for a permanent outdoor installation of thirty-three 8 ½-foot-tall figures for the renowned contemporary art collection of Giuliano Gori at Villa Celle in Pistoia, Italy.

While Abakanowicz's hollowed-out figures express the violation of the body, she has also addressed the abuses of nature. In the late 1980s, she began working with gnarled, misshapen trees found in the Mazury Lakes region north of Warsaw. Rejected by commercial foresters because of their idiosyncratic shapes, the trunks were reclaimed by

Abakanowicz as sculptures. Reshaped with chainsaw and axe, some were fitted with steel blades while others had their severed ends wrapped in cloth or encased in metal. Called *War Games*, these enormous tree carcasses resemble both amputees and battering rams or torpedoes. They are at once weapons and victims, evoking the forces of nature and its fate in an exploitative culture: The sculptures seem to represent the casual violence perpetrated against nature as the world's great forests face oblivion.

The same sense of ambiguity is what makes Abakanowicz's *Hand-like Trees* so compelling. They are at once human and vegetal. They combine the forms of blasted tree trunks with clenched or abbreviated hands; they simultaneously resemble torsos. Each sculpture has a vertical aperture on one side like an absent spine revealing a darkened cavity within. Read as trees or as torsos, the sculptures appear to have severed limbs; as hands, they reveal truncated digits. Just as she does

69

with her figures, Abakanowicz achieves expressiveness in these sculptures through the use of oppositions. The roughly textured, skinlike exterior contrasts with a skeletal interior. The forms appear to grow and mutate, yet they are brutally cropped.

For the installation of her *Hand-like Trees* in Charleston, Abakanowicz chose one of the most visible and most exposed landscapes in the city, and one of the most freighted with history. She selected the high wall at the Battery, on the harbor adjacent to White Point Garden and across the street from a memorial to the Confederate defenders of Charleston. The place has been witness to human and natural calamity alike:

A windswept spot that has received the brunt of many a hurricane, it has also seen more than its fair share of armed conflict. It is one of the places where Charlestonians gathered to watch the attack on Fort Sumter that began the Civil War; it was fortified with earthworks during the subsequent naval blockade and bombing of the city. In this particular setting, the sculptures took on additional connotations. More than one observer noted that they called to mind the ancient oaks of White Point Garden after they were shorn of leaves and branches in 1989's Hurricane Hugo. They also suggest amputees—like the living dead who were the harvest of so many Civil War battles.

But the combination of brutality and hope evident in so many of Abakanowicz's sculptures is apparent in these works as well. They evoke pollarded trees, cut back fiercely in the winter to produce a vigorous, dense growth of new branches in the spring. The *Hand-like Trees* would appear to express dormancy both in the seasons of the spirit and of nature. But they likewise embody the promise of rebirth.—J.B.

1. Quotations from Magdalena Abakanowicz's autobiography *Portrait X 20*, are taken from Michael Brenson, "Survivor Art," *New York Times Magazine*, November 29, 1992, 47-54.

Herb Parker

Enclosure; Vista

White Point Garden at King and
South Battery Streets

Herb Parker's *Enclosure; Vista* was a two-story grass temple, nestled in the grand oaks and lawn of Charleston's White Point Garden. "Ideally, I wanted people to just happen upon it, and for the experience to be tranquil and thoughtful," Parker remarked. "I hoped my work would touch a universal, primeval spot in the human soul." White Point Garden is a popular park with numerous landmarks and an expansive view of the rivers and harbor. It draws many visitors and residents, and their sustained curiosity about *Enclosure; Vista* attested to the success of Parker's ambition.

Since 1983, Parker has been creating environmental sculptures throughout the United States and Canada as well as overseas, including both architectural forms and cavelike structures. "Human/Nature" provided the first opportunity for the artist to build a piece in Charleston, where he presently lives and works as an associate professor of sculpture at the College of Charleston. Like much of his recent outdoor work, *Enclosure;*

Vista was a living edifice built of sod and earth over a steel armature. The piece operated on several levels: most immediately as a cool, shady habitation, smelling of grass and rich earth, which elicited the sensory delights and feelings of tranquillity that an observer might experience in a verdant, sheltering landscape. But the work also addressed the city's architectural context, and established analogies between cycles of nature and the growth and decay of buildings.

Enclosure; Vista was designed as an open, rectangular temple measuring 17 feet long, 19 feet wide, and 15 feet high, surrounded by a simple wrought-iron framework. The temple incorporated thirty-four exterior and thirteen interior columns covered by a sloped roof and a smaller second story. Two layers of sod interspersed with earth covered the steel grid frame of the roof; stacked squares of sod over steel pipes formed blocky columns. *Enclosure; Vista* marked a departure from Parker's previous work in two respects. It was the artist's

first use of wrought iron, and it created a larger and more focused interior space than his earlier projects.

Entering through iron gates, the visitor traversed the sod house through a colonnaded passageway and found a set of stairs made of rammed earth. At the platform at the top of the stairs, the viewer stood partially within a cupolalike enclosure, a smaller version of the first level, with short columns supporting a sloped roof. This vantage point offered framed views in all directions: into the park, over the harbor and onto the surrounding residences. It was here—inside, looking out—that the seemingly contradictory terms of the project's title were reconciled.

Several elements of *Enclosure; Vista* related to Charleston and its cultural and environmental traditions. Relatively small in scale, the work suggested the quality of intimacy and enclosure that is characteristic of the city's historic homes and gardens. Its colonnaded form echoed the wraparound porticoes of planta-

tion homes and the columned verandas of Charleston houses. The structure was entirely fenced in wrought iron in emulation of the city s ornamental ironwork—notably evident in the gardens directly across the street. The iron framework was topped by a decorative finial shaped like a pineapple, the ubiquitous motif of Southern hospitality, echoing the one at the top of the 1905 wooden pavilion in the center of the park. For Parker, the iron was also "a means of controlling, the only somewhat stable element. It signified keeping people out by allowing people in." The building was thus symbolic of Charleston itself, inviting yet restrictive, its alluring natural and historical environment poised in a fragile, limited balance with the explosive contemporary growth of population, tourism, and commercial development in the area.

Parker conceived of the natural materials and the evolving and ephemeral qualities of his structure as "metaphors for architecture and civilization as well as our interaction

with nature, a microcosm of societal growth and decay." *Enclosure; Vista* incorporated archaic features, such as the modified temple plan with two rows of columns and an inner chamber, which made reference to ancient Greek architecture. The rammed earth construction of the stairs likewise employed a building process more than 5,000 years old, one which experienced a revival in Charleston during the early twentieth century. Rammed earth consists of a mixture of seventy percent sand and thirty percent clay pounded in layers into wooden forms. The resulting material was extremely durable and sustained considerable pedestrian traffic during the course of the exhibition. *Enclosure; Vista* continued to grow and change over the summer, the grass becoming longer and shaggier, obscuring the iron frame, and giving a sense of animation to the structure.

Like his earlier environmental work, *Enclosure; Vista* combined historical precedents with theoretical concepts about natural and man-made systems. As Parker explained, "for me, the work served as an ephemeral memento of the power of nature and as an affirmation of the continuum of systems within the natural order." But he also insisted that the use of common, organic materials to create an inviting, natural structure was a primary concern. He confirms that "one thing I like about outdoor work is that you don't have to be a knowledgeable art critic or connoisseur to appreciate it; there are many levels. Often, people relate more to the materials and the structure. They don't have to read deep meaning." As a writer for the *Atlanta Constitution* observed, "Most folks seemed entertained by the oddity of being in a house made of lawn," especially one that was miniaturized in scale and framed like an ornamental birdcage.[1]

Born in 1953 in Elizabeth City, North Carolina, Parker received his B.F.A. and M.F.A. degrees from East Carolina University. He acknowledges the influence of the early generation of earth artists such as Robert Smithson and Richard Long, as well as Hans Haacke's theories of "systems manipulation." Parker also refers to the nature philosophy of Emerson and Thoreau as a foundation for his conception of landscape, particularly the sense of "becoming one with nature, creating an environment that has the feeling of completeness and self-sufficiency, and gives an awareness of the cycles of nature and the passage of time."

In the past fifteen years, Parker has executed more than thirty outdoor installations in sites throughout the United States, Canada, and Italy, including the Toronto Sculpture Garden, ArtPark in Lewiston, New York, Fairmount Park in Philadelphia, the Contemporary Arts Center in New Orleans, and the South Carolina Botanical Garden at Clemson University. —R.K.

1. Catherine Fox, "Landscapes Speak in Spoleto," *Atlanta Constitution*, May 28, 1997, D7.

Patrick Dougherty

The Path of Least Resistance

Washington Park at Broad
and Meeting Streets

Patrick Dougherty's *The Path of Least Resistance* moved through Charleston's Washington Park much the same way that people do—by shortcut. In the southwest quadrant of the oak-lined square, he observed a well-trodden path cutting across the grass, circumventing the formal brick walkways that define this 1824 city park. "Landscape architects call such an alternate footpath a 'desire line.' It struck me as visible evidence of human nature," Dougherty remarked. The live oak trees and path became the generating elements of a four-part sculpture woven from maple saplings: "I wanted to fill the open space between the hard line of the path and the great curved lines of the live oak trees. My challenge was to take something thin and narrow and create an illusion."

For many viewers, *The Path of Least Resistance* was approached by a "teaser" piece on the Meeting Street sidewalk flanking the park, where a 12-foot-high vertical tower spiraled upward over the iron fence of the park and made two loops through the branches of the live oak tree. The maple saplings then curled down to the ground, creating a hivelike structure that could be walked through. The next component mirrored this piece in shape, but offered a turn off the footpath with an opening on one side. The remaining tunnel of woven maple was the longest and most complex, with several openings along its curving path and above it in the trees. A visitor entering Washington Park from Broad Street would encounter this piece first, and take the path toward Meeting Street. Each part of *The Path of Least Resistance* was integrated with a tree, using the pattern of branches to create intricate spaces and framed views. Overall, the piece swept through the park like a cyclone, leaping over the fence, spinning through the limbs and touching down around massive trunks.

As with his other installations, Dougherty proceeded from a general design concept. Yet the sculpture evolved during its creation on location, integrating with the unique features of Charleston's natural, built, and social environments. His sculptures are created entirely by hand using native materials, such as the maple saplings harvested locally for this piece. "Saplings are plentiful and renewable; they have an inherent way of joining, of snapping together and holding in place." Dougherty has likened the formal aspects of his work to drawing in space. The sculptures are constructed by driving larger branches into the ground, then filling in with the pliant, narrower saplings, using the tensile strength of the material to create dynamic, linear patterns and structural flow.

In his work, Dougherty seeks to re-create a sensation of simple joy and play in nature that is as basic as his own (or our) experience of exploring the woods as a child. His sculptures offer places of discovery and sanctuary in a naturally conceived environment, even as they evoke ancient shelters and building techniques. In this regard *The Path of Least Resistance* was similar to Herb Parker's *Enclosure; Vista*.

Dougherty's project in Charleston had some unplanned local resonances as well. The work was a monumental variation on the weaving of grass baskets, a tradition continued by African-American women nearby at the corner of Meeting and Broad streets. And his industriousness was an amusing contrast to the yellow-crowned night herons, who painstakingly build their nests every year in the trees of Washington Park.

By choosing Washington Park as the site for *The Path of Least Resistance*, Dougherty sought to place himself and his work in a highly public location, which he considers fundamental to his objective of stimulating a lively cultural exchange between his sculpture and interested observers. The park is situated directly behind the intersection of Meeting and Broad, commonly called the "Four Corners of the Law" (symbolizing federal, state, city and God's law, as represented, respectively, in the buildings of the post office, the former state house, city hall, and St. Michael's Church

on each corner). At the center of Charleston's business and legal district, this square is heavily used by residents and tourists alike, a situation which the artist noted during his early visits to the city. During the three-week period that he was in the park building *The Path of Least Resistance*, Dougherty eagerly responded to the curiosity of viewers with a discussion of his art, its processes and materials, and his participation in the "Human/Nature" exhibition. "I get to talk to people, and this does a lot for art in general. It demystifies it and makes it more comprehensible to the viewer. You learn how it's done, and then perhaps you find you like it," he remarks. Dougherty's sociability generally insures the popularity of his work while he is making it. Long after he has gone, however, his sculptures continue to exert their appeal through sinuous form and hand-crafted appearance.

Dougherty was born in Oklahoma in 1945 and raised in North Carolina. He earned a B.A. in English from the University of North

Carolina and an M.A. from the University of Iowa. He started his career as a hospital administrator, but returned to Chapel Hill in 1975 to work as a carpenter and stone mason while studying sculpture and art history. Inspired by building his own home in 1979, Dougherty began to devote himself fully to sculpture, progressing from individual pieces to the temporary large-scale environments for which he has earned a distinguished international reputation.

Since his first one-man show in 1983, Dougherty has executed more than a hundred site-specific works for museums, public places, and sculpture gardens in the United States and abroad. In form and content, these installations have varied from the monumental reclining figure he created in 1994 for the Krakamarken Sculpture Park in Denmark, to *Sittin' Pretty*, a freestanding architectural structure made for Clemson University's South Carolina Botanical Garden in 1996. Like *The Path of Least Resistance*, many explore the movement of forms through space and consist of several parts. Frequently, he will incorporate narrative, conceptual, or ironic associations, which are revealed through the interplay of form with his choice of titles. For example, *Family Trees,* created for the Katonah Museum in New York, featured vertical cocoonlike elements attached to actual trees in the courtyard. The real trees resembled sturdy parents and the woven cocoons snuggled like children; the branches of attachment appeared to be an embrace. In this case, the title helped convey the installation's lyrical, animated sensibility.

Dougherty has consistently employed woven saplings as his medium, preferring maple for its color and flexibility. He has also used woods that are indigenous to different sites, including willow, ash, and mulberry. In 1991, while participating in a National Endowment for the Arts Creative Arts Fellowship, he collaborated with the Japanese landscape architect Tsutomu Kasai on *Intricate Loops,* a bamboo piece for the courtyard of the Kakitogawa Museum of Art outside of Tokyo.

Extremely prolific, Dougherty executes about ten large-scale sculptural projects each year. He identifies his work as "creative problem solving," which stirs his imagination and the imaginations of his audience. For each commission, he develops an approach that integrates materials, form, and line with the physical and social characteristics of a specific environment. To this, he brings his personal engagement with the site. The results have been successful and considerably varied, while the process has been refined to create an impressive body of temporary outdoor sculptures.

—R.K.

Philip Simmons and Pearl Fryar

The Heart Garden at the Philip Simmons Garden

St. John's Reformed Episcopal Church
91 Anson Street

Charleston's master blacksmith, the octogenarian African-American artist Philip Simmons, has always brought an inspired vision to the creative ironwork for which he is nationally celebrated. Although he practices a craft that is pervasive in Charleston, Simmons is unusual in drawing many of his motifs from local flora and fauna—trees, fish, and birds. "Maybe I can arrive something from my mind just by nature, looking at nature," he explains. "Sometimes it might be a tree. We got palm trees around Charleston. You get up on the morning, you look at nature. Then you look at other things around Charleston. Then you stop and think and you say, 'Someday I'll make this or the other thing.'" [1]

Simmons' most recent contribution to the metalworking tradition in Charleston is an expansion of his garden at St. John's Reformed Episcopal Church, a project begun in 1992 by the Philip Simmons Foundation as a tribute to his achievements. Simmons had already created a gate and fence enclosing a por-

tion of this landscape when the "Human/ Nature" exhibition provided the impetus to develop another permanent garden in back of the church. The Spoleto Festival was able to enlist Pearl Fryar, a self-taught African-American topiary artist from Bishopville, South Carolina, to collaborate on this project, combining their extraordinary visions and artistry in a garden that permanently enriches the Charleston community.

Simmons designed the tall entry gates with elaborate scrollwork using the heart-and-cross motif of his earlier ironwork on the site. The hearts are formed from a series of scrolls that coil inward to the center line of the heart, giving the design the dynamic visual energy that is a feature of much of Simmons' work. Actively patterned and curvilinear, the hearts are juxtaposed to the simpler spokes of the gate and the cross that rises from the central junction of each heart.

For an aperture in the new stucco and brick wall enclosing the garden, Simmons cre-

ated an ornamental grill depicting a schematic vision of Charleston. He calls the piece *The Holy City*, a moniker sometimes applied to Charleston because of its many churches. In this composition, the peninsula is rendered in large scrolls that form a pear shape, while a border of regular, undulating curves represents the Ashley and Cooper rivers. A diamond at the center of the composition represents church steeples; it is flanked by two single houses with peaked roofs. Together they denote some of the most characteristic features of Charleston views.

Simmons was born in 1912 on Daniel Island, South Carolina, and came to live permanently in Charleston in 1925. Although located just across the Cooper River from Charleston, Daniel Island was a remote rural community isolated from its urban neighbor. Simmons began his craft as an apprentice to the blacksmith Peter Simmons. He started working independently in 1935, at a time when ironworking was declining as automo-

biles replaced horses and wagons and manufactured metal products superseded handcrafted work. By 1939, Simmons began to discover a market for decorative ironwork that had emerged with the restoration and preservation of Charleston's historic homes and buildings. "I had a vision and I could sculpture a lot of things on the anvil itself," he remarks. "I studied wrought iron around Charleston. I knew I could make it, and it set me a new pace after blacksmithing became a lost art."[2]

Since mid-century, Simmons has produced more than 250 examples of finely wrought ornamental gates, fences, and architectural elements throughout Charleston, including the large *Snake Gates* for the Christopher Gadsden House on East Bay Street. These feature renderings of the rattlesnake image derived from the "Don't Tread on Me" Revolutionary-era flag designed by Gadsden. Among his other works, Simmons is especially proud of the *Star and Fish Gate*, which

was executed on site at the Smithsonian's Festival of American Folklife on the Mall in Washington, D.C. Now in the collection of the National Museum of American History, this gate portrays complex and unusual forms such as a star within a star and a lively, spot-tail bass created to demonstrate the range and skill of Simmons's craft to national audiences. As a result of his work, Simmons earned a National Heritage Fellowship from the National Endowment for the Arts in 1982, the first of this kind of award to be granted to an individual.

Pearl Fryar brought his distinctive talent to the Philip Simmons Garden in the creation of fantastical topiaries and stone-inlaid walkways around four parterres. To serve as the centerpiece of the garden, Fryar brought a 5-foot-tall Japanese holly from his garden in Bishopville, which he had sculpted into a design of interlocking hearts over the previous five years. Continuing this motif, he placed new topiaries—a Leyland cypress and a colum-

nar juniper—along the back wall and side of the church. Bricks, marble chips, and decorative stepping stones, including heart-shaped pavers, were laid in a cruciform concrete walk to create whimsical images and patterns. The beds were bordered with yaupon hollies and planted with topiaries of juniper and compacted hollies formed into spirals and pompoms. In a new departure for Fryar, he also experimented with weeping cedars shaped into abstractions on plastic arches. For its initial season, the garden was completed with flowers and several Noisette roses, a class of roses developed in Charleston in the late eighteenth century. The garden will mature over time, as topiaries fill out under the care of the artist and a maintenance crew trained by him.

Pearl Fryar was born in North Carolina in 1939 and graduated from North Carolina Central University. A full-time, down-the-line serviceman for American National Can Corporation, he has brought singular energy and dedication to topiary art, which he pursues on his days off. Fryar began his garden in 1984, when he became intrigued with a topiary plant found at a local nursery. He developed his skills independently, freely exploring unconventional techniques and designs, particularly in the organic abstractions that he considers the most creative aspect of his work. He had modest ambitions at first: He recounts that he began his topiaries because he wanted to win the yard-of-the-month award from his local garden club, a distinction he received in 1987. Since then, he has transformed his 3-acre garden in Bishopville into a spectacular visionary landscape of hundreds of topiary shrubs and trees, pruned and trained into free-form abstract sculptures as well as hearts, fish, and mushrooms. Two long borders are planted with cypresses and blue spruces that ascend in totemlike towers of stacked ovals and dishlike forms. These alternate with low junipers that loop and sprawl in serpentine motion. Other plants, including oaks and hollies, are in varying states of development. Fryar also created elaborate stone and masonry borders and walkways in this garden.

Fryar has gained national recognition for his work, with feature articles in publications such as *Garden Design* and *Fine Gardening*, and television coverage on P.B.S.'s *Victory Garden*. He has been commissioned to create topiaries for public and private gardens, including the South Carolina State Museum in Columbia.

R.K.

Project credits:
Landscape architect: Sheila Wertimer.
Masonry construction by Robert Johnson.

1. John Michael Vlach, *Charleston Blacksmith: The Work of Philip Simmons* (Athens, Georgia: University of Georgia Press, 1981), 92.

2. Tom Watson, "Philip Simmons," *Art and Antiques*, March 1994, 128.

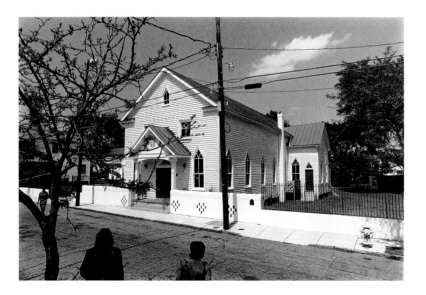

Martha Jackson-Jarvis

Rice, Rattlesnakes, and Rainwater

St. Luke's Reformed Episcopal Church
60 Nassau Street

Although she grew up in Virginia and Pennsylvania and now lives in Washington, D.C., Martha Jackson-Jarvis was no stranger to coastal culture even before she was invited to participate in "Human/Nature." In 1989, she served as the visual arts consultant for Julie Dash's film *Daughters of the Dust*, about a sea island family taking leave of their ancestral home in the early years of the twentieth century. This was Jackson-Jarvis's first encounter with Gullah culture, the distinctive blend of African, Caribbean, and American traditions that lingers, albeit in dwindling measure, along the South Atlantic seaboard. "There was something so haunting about the environment itself, also its history," she recalls. She particularly remembers attending a ceremony at the Penn School on St. Helena Island near Beaufort, founded after the Civil War to educate freed slaves. "Everyone was dressed in red and white, the colors of school. An elderly woman rose to speak and asked, 'Where do you think these colors come from? They are

the colors of Shango, the West African god of the thunder.' I was struck by the fact that there were these carryovers that were just there, part of everyday life, but with roots in Africa."

The experience made Jackson-Jarvis an avid student of coastal African-American culture. She immersed herself in books on the subject, including *Black Majority*, Peter H. Wood's study of colonial South Carolina; *Before Freedom, When I Just Can Remember*, twenty-seven oral histories of former South Carolina slaves; Leland Ferguson's *Uncommon Ground*, an archaeology of early African America, and Phyllis Galembo's *Divine Inspiration*, about Afro-Caribbean religious traditions. From these sources and others, she learned about the survivals of African culture in the New World, including distinctive house types, basketweaving, and pottery. She came to know the tradition of cemetery decoration, in which everyday materials associated with the deceased are placed around the grave to serve as emblems of communication with the world

beyond. And she learned of the related phenomenon of yard dressing, in which cast-off materials are recycled as decoration with similar spiritual resonances—the objects are sanctified by the labor of those who owned or made them.

In subtle ways, these ideas have informed Jackson-Jarvis's work ever since. Her principal medium is glazed and fired clay, but she often collages salvaged materials into her elaborate ceramic objects and installations, including fragments of plates or tiles that belonged to family and friends. "The objects contain memories, life histories," she explains. "The spirit of the person is stored there." The discovery of a trove of antique Venetian mosaic glass at an estate sale in Pennsylvania in 1989 inspired a shift toward an even richer use of materials—not merely clay, crockery, and glass, but copper, coal, slate, and other stones as well. At the same time, the range of her imagery expanded to encompass both abstract shapes and representational ele-

ments, including plant forms, serpents, and fish. This physical elaboration was a metaphor for the fecundity of nature, a way of exploring both the wondrousness and the fragility of creation.

Jackson-Jarvis's concern for nature was expressed most pointedly in a suite of seven massive, tapered ceramic and mosaic sculptures made in the early 1990s. Collectively called *Last Rites*, the sculptures were meant to suggest coffins or ancient sarcophagi. Each sarcophagus had a different theme; four of them were intended as eulogies for the basic elements of life, increasingly imperiled by mushrooming population and industrial pollution: earth, air, plants, and water. Each was suggestively embellished. The one that honored plants, for example, was layered with botanical forms in mosaic, while the tribute to water was predominantly blue and piled high with cast ceramic fish.

While Jackson-Jarvis had worked previously with ideas about nature, the commission

for "Human/Nature" was her first landscape project. Drawing on her familiarity with coastal culture, she planned from the outset to create a testimonial to the African-American experience of the low-country landscape. She wanted the project located in one of Charleston's predominantly black neighborhoods; knowing that she would touch on both the spiritual and material dimensions of landscape, she looked for a protected, even sanctified site. When she saw the churchyard at St. Luke's Reformed Episcopal on the city's east side, she recognized that it fit these requirements. It was also the right scale for the garden she was planning, which would feature mosaic and oyster-shell houses, rain barrels covered with ceramic fish, and a cross-shaped walk, all enclosed in a wrought-iron fence bearing emblems of Afro-Caribbean deities. To be called *Rice, Rattlesnakes, and Rainwater*, the project would explore the physical and religious adaptations of African people in their enforced exile.

The pastor of St. Luke's, Dr. Julius Barnes, and his congregation responded enthusiastically, if a bit quizzically, to the artist's plans and invited her to go ahead. Their reservations grew deeper before they were allayed. "At first, I was a little concerned," Dr. Barnes told a reporter from the *New York Times*. "There was mention of old African gods and other things. I wasn't sure how my people would respond."[1] When the walk first appeared, the congregation saw it had a rattlesnake at the crossing, which they initially took to be an emblem of evil. But Jackson-Jarvis was able to resolve their concerns. The rattlesnake, she explained, was an emblem of the wild landscape encountered and cleared by slaves. The snake is also a universal symbol of healing, used in medical insignia; it reappears in the staffs at the back of the garden. As to the emblems of West African deities found elsewhere in the fence, she explained they were suggestive of the beliefs that slaves brought with them from Africa; they repre-

sented the forces they might have invoked to shelter them in a strange land. At the gate of the garden, for example, is an abstracted shield composed of the reversing spirals and spear associated with Ogun, which guards against danger. As the god of tools and blacksmithing, it is Ogun who is believed to open pathways in a new place, "to make a way out of no way," as the artist put it. The lightning bolts and arrows in the central panels at either side of the garden evoke Shango, the god of thunder who is also associated with agriculture. Near them is the form of a fish, a reference both to Yemaya, the female deity of the oceans, and Ochun, god of fresh water, plants, and medicine, who is also invoked in the serpent staffs. At the corners of the fence, bottle trees offer additional protection. A common feature in vernacular gardens across the South, they are believed to trap or confuse evil spirits with their flashing reflections.

Within the fence, landscape elements receive a more localized expression. The rain barrels suggest the necessity of collecting fresh water on islands surrounded by brackish estuaries. They are embellished with glazed ceramic fish cast from species found in coastal waters, including red snapper, red hind, pompano, and flounder; some of these fish reappear on the houses, which are meant to evoke modest slave dwellings. The houses are encrusted with the shells of oysters, another local food; they also carry the mosaic image of the rice plant. People from West Africa were especially prized because of their familiarity with rice cultivation; their knowledge was ironically a cause of their enslavement. The houses also carry enormous mosaic images of mosquitos, carriers of the malaria that plagued master and slave alike, though the

presence of the sickle-cell trait in some Africans made them resistant to the disease.

In all, Jackson-Jarvis explains, *Rice, Rattlesnakes, and Rainwater* expressed "the power of landscape to affect our lives. It pays homage to the many thousands gone and celebrates the wit and ingenuity of the survivors." It struck a chord with many of its neighbors. "People are very excited about it," Dr. Barnes told the *New York Times* reporter during the festival. "The church has had more visitors in the last few weeks than it has ever had. It's as though a spark has been lit in the community." With an extraordinary range of materials and images, Jackson-Jarvis created a vibrant tribute to the material and spiritual history of African-American culture in the low country.
—J.B.

Project credits:

Wrought-iron fence fabricated by Rick Avrett, Ole Charleston Forge. Masonry walk by Albert Allston.

1. Dr. Julius Barnes, quoted in Rick Lyman, "New Parts of Town for Spoleto Festival," *New York Times*, June 2, 1997, B1.

Mary Lucier

House by the Water

Pedestrian alley between
Hutson and John Streets

The setting is the darkened interior of an old brick warehouse off an alley in the commercial district along Charleston's upper King Street. In the center of a room about 35 by 50 feet long and 35 feet high is a single architectural structure, angled so that its walls face the corners of the room. It is a simplified house on stilts about 18 feet high with white siding and a metal roof, enclosed in a chain-link fence and faintly illuminated from within by two blue bulbs. It suggests a weather station. Images flicker on all sides of the structure, emanating from video projectors hung from the roof. From any vantage point, only two walls of the house are visible at a time, but the images appear to be perfectly synchronized. At times, they follow each other around the building; at others they offer multiple perspectives on the same scene, creating a fragmented narrative. Sound fills the space. Most of it seems to be derived from taped conversations, which are sometimes intelligible. But at other points, the sound is slowed down, processed, or amplified, creating a distorted, ghostly effect. At moments, the sound seems to have a directional character, starting first in one speaker, then the next. Drawn by the movement of image and sound, you revolve around the house, assembling the parts of this puzzle into a composite mental picture.

The sequence of audiovisual experiences is baffling at first. Sunlight glimpsed through the branches of trees shines from the walls of the structure, accompanied by the songs of birds. Choppy water is seen close-up, with the sound of waves breaking against the bow of a boat. The interior of a grand but deteriorated house comes next, along with a spoken narrative about enlarging the slave quarters to shelter more servants. A girl in a white dress pirouettes in front of a full-length nineteenth-

century portrait of a woman in a formal gown; the girl's long twirling skirt fades to become the ghostly radar image of a hurricane making landfall on the Carolina coast. The room goes black.

When the images return, we are looking down the corridor of a weatherbeaten dwelling, presumably the slave quarters mentioned in the narrative. Two figures appear in sequence: an African-American man and woman, both in the nineteenth-century clothing of domestic servants, run separately down the corridor in slow motion to the prolonged and amplified sound of pounding footfalls. As they approach the camera, they vanish. On a contemporary street, the camera passes small, fragile-looking houses and waving black men. Back in the interior of the slave dwelling, the man and woman read in separate but simultaneous scenes projected on opposite sides of the structure. We see the Bible over their shoulders, open to the book of Isaiah. As the camera zooms in on the page, we make out some of the text from Chapter 41, verse 17: "When the poor and needy seek water and there is none, and their tongue is parched with thirst, I the Lord will answer them, I the God of Israel will not forsake them." Then waves crash against a coastline, driven by furious winds. The radar image of a hurricane appears again, this time in color. The walls of the house go dark. After a few seconds, sunlight appears, and the cycle begins again.

In brief, such was the experience of Mary Lucier's multimedia installation *House by the Water*. It included footage shot in Charleston—in the street and on the estuary—with radar and video images of hurricanes that have ravaged the city. It also featured vignettes with white and black actors produced at the historic Aiken-Rhett House, an unrestored ante-

bellum mansion maintained by the Historic Charleston Foundation. Lucier taped both the main house and the slave quarters, both empty and animated with actors in period costumes who evoked the lives of people who once lived there. While exploring the connections between social history and the environment, *House by the Water* also dramatized the perils of living close to the primal forces of nature.

A pioneer in the relatively new field of video art, Lucier has been creating multimedia installations since 1973. Like *House by the Water*, many address the experience of landscape. *Dawn Burn* (1975), for example, composed of seven monitors in a freestanding arc, was made by pointing the camera at the sunrise every morning for seven days and creating a solar burn in the video tube, while *Ohio at Giverny* (1983) was videotaped both in the artist's home state and in Monet's renowned garden in France.

Lucier has also worked with architectural forms before. For a 1993 installation called *Oblique House (Valdez)*, for example, Lucier designed a rectangular plasterboard structure with a peaked roof 23 feet high. Inside, monitors in each corner played interviews with four residents of Valdez, Alaska, who had survived various disasters, including an earthquake that flattened the town in 1964 and the notorious oil spill in 1989. These monitors were interactive—motion sensors turned them on as viewers approached. Overhead, images of landscape were projected on the ceiling, inverting inside and out, sky and ground. Cataclysm was presented here in both its human and natural forms in recognition of the fact that culture, like nature, can be both creative and destructive.

As suggested by these synopses, Lucier typically ventures far beyond simple depictions of landscape to explore the ways that humans occupy an environment. Like Charles Simonds (see pages 116-121), she has created extended meditations on the body and landscape as different but analogous forms of habi-

tation. *Noah's Raven*, a four-channel laser-disc installation for eight monitors in an arrangement of trees and forklifts beneath a hanging fossil, drew parallels between environmental and bodily health. It juxtaposed the clearing and burning of forests with the body in surgery, enforcing connections between the scarring of land and of flesh. The installation registered her response to the destruction of the Amazon rain forest, "which I think is one of the most futile exercises on the face of this planet." But it was also made during the time that her mother was fighting a three-and-a-half-year battle with cancer. "I wanted to look at scarring as a common issue that could be seen as benign or malignant. Some scars are beneficial in that a disease has been cured. Others are the scars of destruction. So I looked at the body and I looked at the landscape with that duality in mind."[1]

Duality was also a pronounced part of *House by the Water*. The installation contrasted inside and outside, shelter and vulnerability,

beauty and terror. The house provided both the basic structure and the dominant metaphor for the project. It was present both as a literal object and as an imaginative space. An actual house, in good condition, stood before us in the warehouse, but another, aged and worn, was represented in the video images. We saw the house from the outside in the literal construction; we plumbed its interiors in the film. In the warehouse, the house occupied our present; in the video images, it was the repository of memories. We expect houses to offer us shelter, but *House by the Water* presented a structure exposed to fierce storms and grievous loss, represented in hurricanes and vanishing figures.

House by the Water drew other comparisons as well. It contrasted the lives of white and black inhabitants of the house even as it it expressed the connections between psychological experience and the external forces of nature, suggesting the ways that people adapt to the vicissitudes of life. Perhaps most poignantly,

the black couple was seen fleeing, perhaps from the advancing storm, perhaps from a life of involuntary servitude. They were also pictured in a quiet moment, reading the Bible, in a sequence that was recorded almost by chance. "It was my idea that they should read, but their idea to read the Bible." Lucier recalls. "We were really coauthors of the scene." Coincidentally, when Lucier focused in on the book, it was open to the passage in Isaiah in which the Lord promises succor to his people and vengeance on their enemies. "Fear not," an adjacent verse reads, "for I am with you. . . . I will strengthen you, I will help you, I will uphold you with my victorious right hand." While serendipitous, this reference underlined the theme of refuge conveyed by the figures in the house. Portrayed in bondage in a land prone to hurricanes and flooding, they nonetheless knew the prophesy: "I the God of Israel will not forsake them." Their house in this instance was more than a literal dwelling. It became a metaphor for faith, a bulwark—however

battered and frail—against the adversities of nature and culture alike. —J.B.

Project credits:
Producer, camera, off-line editor: Mary Lucier.
Sound composition and processing: Earl Howard.
Performers: Linzy Washington, Karen Washington, Frances Atkins. Production Assistance: Richard Hill and Stacey Chalmers. Installation Construction: Kevin Fisher, Spoleto Scene Shop. Post-production facilities provided through the stand-by program, Broadway Video, New York.

Acknowledgments:
Sean Huston, Channel 2 (WCBD), Charleston.
Peter Dodge, Hurricane Research Division, AOML.
Tom Savage, Historic Charleston Foundation.

1. Mary Lucier, quoted in Nicholas Drake, "Artist Uses Life Experiences as Basis for Mixed-Media Works," *Post and Courier*, May 29, 1997, Spoleto Today (special section), 2.

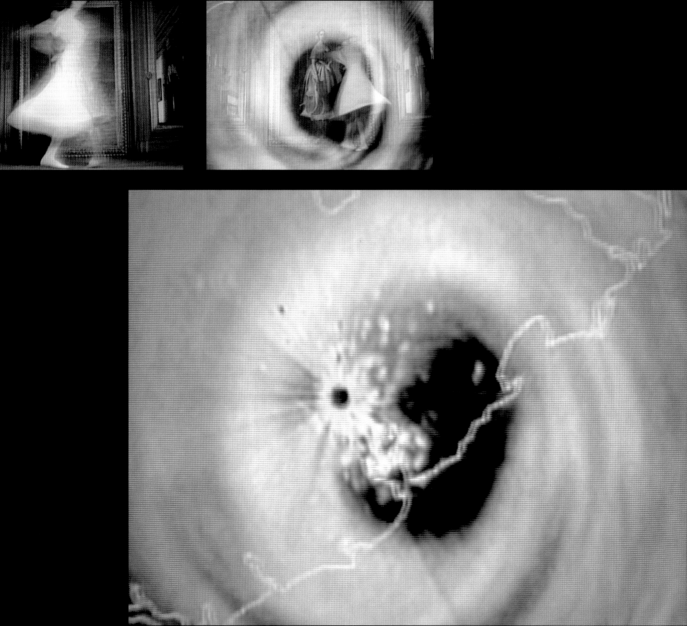

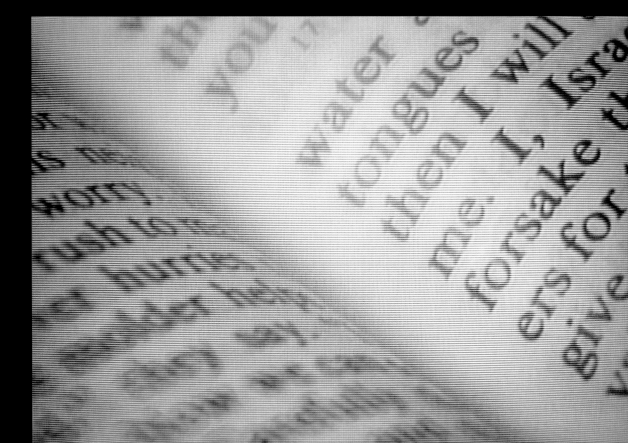

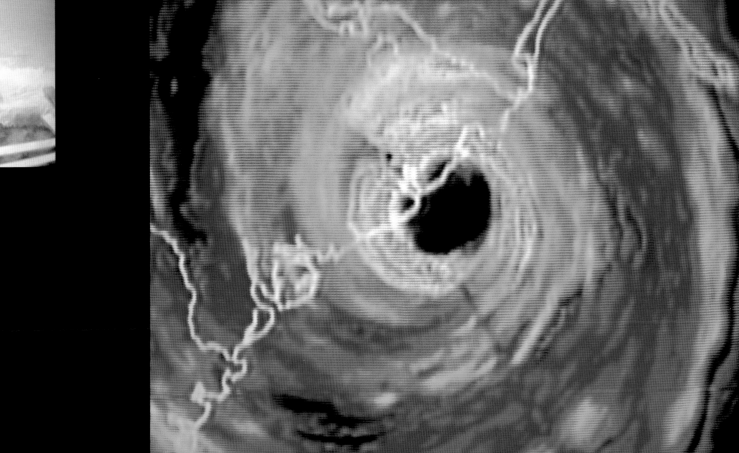

110

Portal to America

High School of Charleston
Rutledge Avenue at Vanderhorst Street

The mural art of the Ndebele, a broad range of ethnic groups found across Zimbabwe and the Transvaal province of South Africa, is designed to announce a family or community celebration, and for Esther Mahlangu's *Portal to America*, the celebrations were many. This three-part painting was dedicated to the South African artist's teachers, her mother, Bakgesile, and her grandmother, Onontrangalu. The work paid tribute to the introduction of Mahlangu's art to the United States, and honored the Spoleto Festival as an international celebration of the arts. Finally, and most poignantly, the artist wished to recognize the historic role of Charleston as port-of-entry for vast numbers of enslaved Africans: Fully one-third to one-half of all slaves transported to the United States in the eighteenth and nineteenth centuries passed through the city.

Portal to America consisted of two vibrantly colored, patterned archways and a mural at the entrance to the now-abandoned High School of Charleston, which were intended to evoke the painted environments of Ndebele homesteads. Painted by Mahlangu with the assistance of her son, Elias, and his wife, Johanna, the three elements lined up under an arcade leading to the door of the old building. The entry arch, which was visible from Rutledge Avenue, was rendered in typical Ndebele style, with geometric forms and bold colors: zigzag lines, triangles, and chevrons, in pink, purple, blue, green, yellow, black, and white. The arched central panel in the courtyard portrayed a number of decorative motifs, including abstract geometric forms and stripes of color that recalled traditional Ndebele blankets. The large mural that covered the doorway to the school featured one of the most common of abstract emblems, the razor blade, called *tshefana*. The bottom portion of this image showed a contemporary version of the earliest technique of wall painting, known as *kguphu* (or "tire tracks"), in which the fingers are dragged through a single color of paint to create designs and textures.[1]

The Ndebele style of mural art emerged at mid-century, when women began to paint the walls of their homes and villages in colors and patterns derived from traditional beadwork designs of the late nineteenth century. The phenomenon seems to have developed as an affirmation of tribal identity in reaction to apartheid rule, and was soon incorporated into domestic and celebratory rituals including weddings and births. The earliest examples were created in the late 1940s at the village of Hartebeestfontein and were distinguished by simple geometric designs and earth pigments, typically made from mud, dung, stone, and charcoal. Ironically, given their oppositional character, these paintings were quickly recognized as a valuable cultural industry by the South African apartheid government, which established "traditional" Ndebele villages as tourist attractions as part of their program to resettle tribal groups in homesteads.

In the decades since the emergence of their art, Ndebele painters have been exceptionally adaptable in their vision, at first incorporating beadwork designs, then elaborating them into overall patterns on the walls of houses, courtyards, and gates. The imagery has developed to include stylized figures and elements derived from urban life, such as the architecture and electric lights of the houses where Ndebele women worked as domestic servants. Painting techniques have likewise evolved from the early use of organic pigments and chicken feather and twig brushes to contemporary acrylic paints and manufactured brushes. Ndebele painting is done freehand,

displaying a remarkable virtuosity in the precise, geometric forms that characterize contemporary work. It remains largely a decorative genre, and many current practitioners disclaim the reading of symbolic or sacred expressions into their art. As Mahlangu explains, "The designs themselves have no special meaning, other than there is a celebration."

House painting is undertaken for the most important ceremony of the Ndebele, *wela*, the male initiation and circumcision ritual. Every four years, young men between the ages of about 15 and 18 are isolated for a period of three months in temporary shelters where they are taught tribal culture, customs, and discipline by appointed elders. *Wela* is the occasion for women to repair the outside walls and entrances of their homes and paint—or repaint—them in the geometric and figurative designs that have evolved over the past half-century.

Young females at the age of puberty are also secluded for a period of three months, when they learn the arts of beadwork, paint-

ing, and the elaborate means of self-adornment practiced among Ndebele women for everyday dress and to indicate age and marital status. The impulse to decorate the domestic environment may have developed from this practice of personal ornamentation, which includes the making and wearing of beaded loin cloths and aprons, *nguba* (marriage blankets), and *dzilla*, the stacks of brass and copper rings worn by married women on their necks, arms, and legs. Beaded necklaces, bracelets, fertility dolls, and decorative items have, like wall painting, served the growing tourist market.

Esther Mahlangu, who was born in 1932 in Middleburg, South Africa, belongs to the people of the Southern Transvaal Ndebele, a group that has maintained their ancestral customs and language despite wars, migration, indentured servitude, and displacement through resettlement.

Mahlangu began painting under her mother's and grandmother's instruction at the age of 10. She began to acquire recognition for her work in 1980, while serving as a resident artist at Botshabelo Museum, an open-air facility designed to present a typical view of Ndebele culture, and while working for the city council of Middleburg. By 1989, she became internationally known when she was invited to France to paint a replica of her house at an international exhibition at the Centre Georges Pompidou in Paris. Mahlangu has been commissioned to paint murals at the Civic Theater in Johannesburg; at the African Festival in Lisbon, Portugal; and at the National Museum of Women in the Arts in Washington, D.C. She was the first woman to be commissioned to paint a BMW car as part of the corporation's official "art car" program, joining the company of Andy Warhol and Robert Rauschenberg, among others.

"When I am painting, my heart is very wide," Mahlangu has said, with a sentiment that seems particularly appropriate to this impressive and joyfully spirited art. —R.K.

1. Ivor Powell, *Ndebele—A People and Their Art* (New York: Cross River Press, 1995), 49.

Charles Simonds

Childhood Follies

Ashley Hall School
172 Rutledge Avenue

Charles Simonds' project for "Human/Nature" was a community affair, involving many of the students and some of the faculty at Ashley Hall, a private school for girls on the grounds of a nineteenth-century estate on Rutledge Avenue. Centered on a Neoclassical villa built about 1816, the estate was acquired in 1879 by a German consul and cotton merchant named G. W. Witte. The grounds still feature several follies built to amuse his six daughters, including a shell house clad in conchs and an artificial cave or grotto overgrown with ficus and vines. The estate was home to a considerable menagerie as well: There were peacocks, monkeys, and horses; the shell house was an aviary for exotic birds; an alligator dubbed Wishy-Washy lived in a fountain; and a tame bear called Frederick lived in the cave.

Simonds discovered the grotto on a visit to Charleston in October and was immediately drawn to it. Caves have played an important role in the history of art: They are the locus of some of the earliest-known paintings and their replicas are a significant element in garden ornamentation beginning in the Renaissance. In many cultures, grottoes are perceived as hallowed. As a Classical topos, they were often identified with sacred springs; in Christian history, they are indelibly linked with the life of Christ (many of the pivotal events in the story of Jesus are believed to have taken place in caves, from the Annunciation and the Nativity to the Entombment). In more recent times, caves have assumed psychological overtones. As a threshold to a hidden world, they can be read as a metaphor for the unconscious.

Simonds' work often involves the projection of subliminal fantasies—sometimes his, sometimes those of his collaborators or his audience. Best known for his creation of an imaginary race of little people, Simonds has built miniature landscapes and tiny ruined dwellings around the world that represent the traces of their civilization. Some of these he fabricates on his own torso, suggesting analogies between the body, landscape, and architecture as different forms of habitation. Others appear on city streets—subtle intrusions into modern life of a seemingly archaic culture more bound to nature.

Though chiefly the product of his own fancy, these little people are at times the armature on which others hang their dreams. Simonds recently worked at the Sainte-Anne Psychiatric Hospital in Paris, site of some well-known encounters between the Surrealists and the mentally ill before World War II, in the quest of the former to explore unconscious sources of creativity.[1] Simonds showed pictures of his work to the patients there, demonstrated how he used clay and sand to make an imaginary place, and fashioned bricks and a wall for them. Then he invited them all to create sculptures of idealized dwelling places or homes, which were assembled into a large tiered form that resembled a wedding cake, becoming a collective image of their individual fantasies.

In the past few years, Simonds has begun to employ figural imagery in his sculptures, with an emphasis on physiognomy—the study of the face as a register of character and emotional experience. He has made several colossal grimacing faces, for example, one with buildings sprouting from its brow, another yoked to its twin. These sculptures might be termed grotesque, a word that owes its origin to the fantastical combinations of human, vegetal, and animal forms found in paintings in the underground vaults or crypts (*grotta*) of ancient Roman houses. These chambers were likewise the inspiration for the bizarre decorations often found in artificial caverns in

117

would make together. They would study the stones, look for suggestive shapes—human and animal forms, for example—and use clay to enhance the latent images. In so doing, he hoped that the cave would provide an opportunity for all of them to experience some of the unconscious origins of the creative impulse. Working with art teacher Meyriel Edge, he showed the students how to play a variation of the game Exquisite Corpse, in which a paper is divided into thirds, and one person draws a head on the top section. Folding it over so the head can not be seen, the first player passes the page on to another to draw the torso; the second player hides his or her work and passes the page on to a third to draw the legs and the feet. The paper is then opened to reveal a composite image made up of individual fantasies.

When Simonds returned to the campus for a week in May, the art classes visited the cave in small groups. He showed them what he was doing and encouraged them to make whatever they liked based on the forms they discovered in the stones. He was aware that he was asking them to rehabilitate forbidden territory, both as a social space and as a site for imaginative activity. "The grotto had been off limits to the students, as some had been caught smoking in there. The place had a reputation for licentiousness," Simonds says. "It looked neglected. The reaction of the students coming in was a mixture of revelation and nervousness." While they all seem to have experienced the space as magical, the creative responses of the students varied. Some simply made clay sculptures that had nothing to do with the shapes discovered in the cave. "But others really let themselves get provoked," Simonds remembers. "The project really allowed them to precipitate out their fantasies."

Simonds himself made an enormous visage with a large tongue and eyes on a branching column just inside the entrance. In the center of the grotto, under an aperture that admitted a little light, he created several contorted faces that appeared to be stacked up on their sides, some suggesting monkeys, others goats and fish. These large elements set the tone for the project and were the easiest to see when you entered the gloomy space. Once your eyes adjusted to the dim light, many other smaller visages appeared. As in the study of physiognomy, these faces were clues to the emotional lives of their makers, some projecting humor, others fear, horror, sadness, even a latent eroticism. The longer you looked, the more the rock walls of the cave came alive with eyes, mouths, and tongues, some evidently made by the artist, others by the students. Lions, mermaids, and bats joined countless unidentifiable and hybrid creatures to animate the stones. At once a social and a psychological landscape, the cave became a place both for collective activity and for the expression of individual psyches. Like a three-dimensional game of Exquisite Corpse, *Childhood Follies* was an occasion to project individual fantasies onto a common ground. It was a portal into the artistic unconscious and the shared world of dreams.

—J.B.

1. On the Surrealists and Sainte-Anne Hospital, see Sarah Wilson, "From the Asylum to the Museum: Marginal Art in Paris and New York, 1938-68" in *Parallel Visions: Modern Artists and Outsider Art* (Los Angeles: Los Angeles County Museum of Art, 1992), 121-26.

2. For more on the grotesque, see E.H. Gombrich, "The Edge of Chaos," in *The Sense of Order: A Study in the Psychology of Decorative Art* (London: Phaidon, 1979).

Renaissance gardens.[2] Though the word grotesque now more commonly denotes the monstrous or the repulsive, Simonds is equally intrigued with its historical connotations of hybridization and incongruous juxtaposition. In his affinity for the grotesque and his fascination with the unconscious, the grotto at Ashley Hall seemed to have been made-to-order for him.

Simonds visited the school in April and briefed the students about his ambitions for the project. He proposed using the weirdly contorted rocks in the grotto's interior to provoke a group of sculptures that he and they

The Low Country

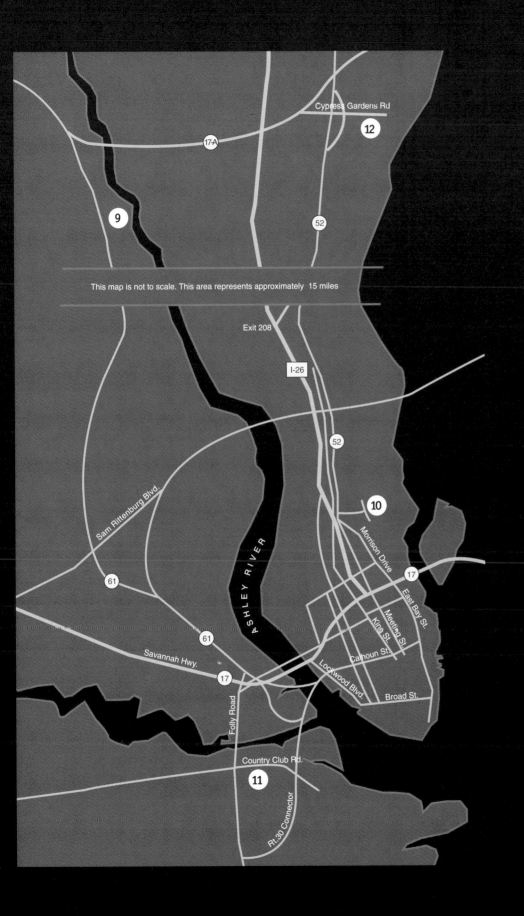

This map is not to scale. This area represents approximately 15 miles

9
Thornton Dial

10
Ronald Gonzalez

11
Martha Schwartz

12
Adriaan Geuze

Thornton Dial

Middleton Place, Ashley River Road
and Gibbes Museum of Art

For thirty years, African-American steelworker Thornton Dial labored in the Pullman boxcar factory in Bessemer, Alabama, initially as a helper and ultimately as a welder. All the while, he was making art: human and animal figures from cast-off metal or carpet; flowers of plastic and rope. When the factory began laying off workers in the early 1980s, he and his sons began making garden furniture in their backyard and called their business Dial's Metal Patterns. In the spirit of his art, lawn chairs and benches grew increasingly elaborate and soon took on the character of freestanding sculptures encrusted with roots, branches, and all manner of found objects. Eventually, these became so numerous that they constituted an example of the informal outdoor studio and exhibition space commonly called the "yard show." By the late 1980s, Dial had also begun producing thickly textured, expressionistic paintings and delicate pastel and watercolor drawings. In the early 1990s, he was being acclaimed as a remarkable talent who had broken through the barriers between contemporary "high" art and self-taught or "outsider" art. As evidence of his stature in these two communities, Dial was given concurrent solo exhibitions in 1993 at New York's New Museum of Contemporary Art and Museum of American Folk Art.

When Dial came to Charleston in the winter of 1997, he was struck by the evidence of the city's abundant African-American history and culture. He learned about Denmark Vesey's 1822 slave rebellion, visited the slave cabins at McLeod Plantation, and met some of the women who carry on a centuries-old tradition weaving sweetgrass into baskets. He saw gates by the noted Charleston blacksmith Philip Simmons and spent an afternoon in his shop, where conversation turned to the sound

Thornton Dial sculptures at Middleton Place

From left to right, *Sticking Together* (1996), *Treeing the Coon* (1995), *Old Country Chair* (1995), and *The Power of the Seat* (1997)

All sculptures gesso and enamel paint on metal and found objects, courtesy of the artist and William S. Arnett, Atlanta

Philip Simmons' Warning:
Beware, There's a Snake at the Gate, 1997

qualities of different metals. Simmons led Dial to a cherished old anvil, hand-forged by his teacher, and began tapping out rhythms, inviting Dial to follow. Soon, the foundry was ringing with a metallic version of call-and-response.

Dial's Charleston experiences became the inspiration for paintings, sculpture, and drawings that were shown at the Gibbes Museum of Art. All reveal the combination of technical mastery and pungent social commentary that is Dial's particular gift. Out wardly colorful and even lighthearted, Dial's creations contain coded messages on troubling matters. They allude to slavery, to differences between white and black and rich and poor, and to the struggle for survival that characterizes life for the less fortunate. Many of them acknowledge landscape as the arena in which social relations are enacted or use metaphors of nature to describe commerce between the races.

Among Dial's Charleston works, the drawings are perhaps the easiest to interpret. The memory of McLeod appears in *The Works of the Slave Quarters*, an image of an antebellum African-American community. A basketmaker is featured in *Working the Sweetgrass*; she is represented in the fluid, elegant lines for which Dial is deservedly renowned. Two of the drawings are tributes to Philip Simmons and include the image of the snake, which is virtually ubiquitous in Dial's Charleston works. Dial borrowed the motif from Simmons' rattlesnake gate at the Gadsden House on East Bay Street, home of the family that included Christopher Gadsden, an officer in the Continental Army and a member of the Continental Congress, and his grandson, James, who negotiated the 1854 Gadsden Purchase. The snake in the gate was a reference to the Revolutionary War-era flag designed by Christopher Gadsden bearing the image of the rattlesnake and the legend "don't tread on me," but Dial adapted the serpent to his own purposes. In his mind, the wrought-iron fences built by craftsmen like Philip Simmons are

symbolic of the barriers erected by whites to exclude black people from political and economic equality. Dial's snake is an emblem of African-Americans who are trying to break through such obstructions and earn a place in society despite the impediments.

The serpent appears most prominently in a sculpture called *Philip Simmons' Warning: Beware, There's a Snake at the Gate*. The figure of Philip Simmons is engulfed by a huge predatory bird, like Jonah in the belly of the whale. From the beak of the raptor hangs the rattlesnake. While both Simmons and the serpent would appear to be vulnerable—the former is on crutches while the latter is at the mercy of the bird—Dial's title suggests that they will ultimately prevail. After all, Dial is not warning us about the power of the hunter but of the hunted.

Dial's Charleston paintings speak to similar themes. *Charleston Gardens: Snake at the Gate* is a Carolina landscape in full bloom, a riot of color and texture under a brilliant sun. But

Old Charleston
(Looking for the Good Life), 1997
mixed media on canvas, 6′ 8″ x 5′ x 3′

Charleston Gardens:
Snake at the Gate, 1997
mixed media on canvas, 6' x 6' x 5"

down one side slithers the snake, fashioned in this instance from a leather belt. *Old Charleston (Looking for the Good Life)* addresses the alienation of African-Americans more explicitly. A figure on a ladder—which could be a self-portrait of Dial—peers over a fence at the rooftops and steeples of the historic town, which have been cut from rusted metal. Dressed in old work clothes, the man appears to be wondering how to climb over the bars and claim a share of the city's rich legacy.

In conjunction with the exhibition at the Gibbes, Dial also loaned a selection of benches and chairs from his yard show in Bessemer. These were installed along the camellia allée and in one of the secret gardens at Middleton Place, the noted plantation on the Ashley River just west of Charleston. Begun in the 1740s and laid out in the grand manner characteristic of European gardens in the late seventeenth and early eighteenth centuries, Middleton Place is one of the oldest designed landscapes in America. Dial's exuberant sculptures, vividly painted and composed of everything from old tires to rope rugs, roots, and string, were a deliberate contrast to the quiet formality and simple geometry of Middleton's gardens. They represented the enduring but infrequently celebrated contributions of African-Americans to the life of the place, which was built and sustained by slaves.

Perhaps most poignant was a piece Dial made especially for this context called *The Power of the Seat (You Can't Do Without Us)*, which features an African-American couple at either end of a bench, the woman with a white baby doll, a plate of food, and a broom, the man with a hammer and a shovel. They seem to be holding up the bench, just as African Americans once provided the foundation for the plantation economy and still make up a great deal of the nation's labor force. *The Power of the Seat* also suggests the special role of chairs as emblems of authority in African-American yard shows. Much as thrones have conventionally been symbols of kingship, chairs are often used in yard shows to elevate the importance of the person or object associated with them.[1]

Dial is alluding in his chairs and benches not to political power, traditionally denied to blacks, but to the more general significance of African-American culture. The conflicts and possibilities of that culture furnished the subjects for others of Dial's sculptures at Middleton Place. Some are representations of scenes from everyday life, such as *Treeing the 'Coon*, where dogs fashioned of yellow-painted carpet hold a porcelain raccoon hostage in a tree. Another, *Cocaine Dog* (a woman hanging from the belly of a beast), addresses the dangers of drug addiction. Perhaps the most subtle and haunting sculpture shown at Middleton evokes the ephemeral nature of memory. *Old Country Chair* is vividly painted on one side, but pale, like fading recollections, on the other. It might serve as a metaphor for all of Dial's work. Speaking across the boundaries of race and class, his sculptures, paintings, and drawings are a forceful effort to protect the legacy of African-American experience from the corrosive effects of time.—J.B.

1. On the role of special seats in African-American yard shows, see Grey Gundaker, "Tradition and Innovation in African American Yards," *African Arts* 26 (April 1993), 58-71.

Top: *Old Country Chair*
Bottom: *The Power of the Seat*
Opposite: *Treeing the Coon*

Ronald Gonzalez

**Scattered Remains:
Corpus, Keeper, Profane**

Magnolia Cemetery and
Gibbes Museum of Art

For more than 150 years, Magnolia Cemetery has been a landscape transformed by art and inspired by the contemplation of death and nature. Dedicated in 1850 on a former plantation along the Cooper River, Magnolia was a picturesque burial ground, envisioned by its founders as a place "where the beauties of nature and the cultivation of taste and art will lend a soothing influence to the grave."[1] As with other American rural cemeteries of the nineteenth century, this "City of the Silent" was artistically conceived as a sanctified landscape for the repose of the dead and as a refuge of devotion for the living, a place to contemplate death as part of the cycles of nature.

A low, semitropical landscape of live oaks, palmettos, and magnolia trees overlooking a view of marsh and river, Magnolia grew to be one of the most impressive rural cemeteries in this country. The grounds were designed with tidal lagoons and inlets, pathways and bridges, and embellished with elaborate grave sites featuring an exotic array of monuments,

including an Egyptian pyramid, a Doric temple, and a Gothic spire. Throughout the cemetery, there are stone obelisks, columns, urns, and crosses with all kinds of ornamentation—carved, draped, wreathed, and scrolled.

The power of this landscape to inspire creative response was explored by the artist Ronald Gonzalez in two elements of his three-part installation, *Scattered Remains.* Overall, the project offered a sculptural meditation on landscape and the body, death and life, and concepts of the sacred and the profane. Magnolia Cemetery was the site of *Corpus* and *Keeper,* while *Profane* was assembled at the Gibbes Museum of Art. All three environments combined figures with various natural materials to create compelling statements about life, death, and resurrection.

For *Corpus,* Gonzalez created a haunting assemblage of twenty-three standing figures enclosed within a fenced grave site on the cemetery grounds. Simultaneously monstrous

and beautiful, the figures were constructed of plaster mixed with marble and granite dust over welded steel and wire armatures. Crosses emerged from faceless heads; partial epithets and emblems derived from Magnolia gravestones were inscribed on the figures to evoke concepts of memory and loss with phrases such as "restore my spirit," and "dying is but going home." Plaster crosses and rusting flower containers (commonly used for grave sites) added to the accumulation of elegiac objects. Ghostly and fragile, the figures exuded a tragic air, standing upon the ground of plaster fragments into which they slowly deteriorated.

While *Corpus* addressed the death of the body, *Keeper* suggested the life of the spirit. Gonzalez conceived of the work as a habitation of angels mounted on the interior walls of the cemetery gatehouse, with a large, caged, feathered creature suspended over water in the middle of the room. The angels were composed of cast plaster and wax-covered

jawbones—images of eternal life made from what the artist called the "jaws of death." Sitting on their mounts, they held shallow votivelike cups, filled with water and tiny floating boats with feathers as sails. A layer of blue glass eyes (twenty thousand of them, relating to the number of grave sites at the cemetery) were poised along the chair rail, watchful and protective. A stuffed fox, mouse and trap, grave marker, and ship were placed around the room. Feathers trailed from an old bathroom, where the sink contained embalming liquid. These elements constituted an interior landscape to mirror the bird and animal life on the lagoons outside, conveying a sense of entropy and fallenness, using the feathers that are so prominently scattered over the grounds of the cemetery. As an accumulation of details, *Keeper* offered mixed and layered allusions to predators and prey, custody and captivity, life, death, and spirituality, all conceived within a realm intimately related to the cemetery and its natural setting.

Isolated within a gallery at the Gibbes Museum, *Profane* served as a contrast and companion to the sanctified world of gatehouse and cemetery. Approached from a long hallway, *Profane* drew the viewer into a hot-red room with a large, central cage of bones. A recessed moat around the cage brought a watery, organic landscape indoors, echoing the incorporation of the cage and water in *Keeper*. Two large figures rising from mounds of jawbones and animal teeth occupied sentrylike positions along the back wall, while numerous smaller devils and an assortment of skull-like heads were mounted on the other walls. Made of cast and burned plaster, teeth, bones, wax, and paint, with scarred surfaces and raw, exposed layers, the sculptures expressed the visceral, profane qualities of carnality and physical corruption. Like Gonzalez's other figures, they seemed to exist on a border between life and death. The effect was searing, in sharp contrast to the reassuring presentation of death and resurrection in nature seen at Magnolia Cemetery.

Ronald Gonzalez was born in Binghamton, New York in 1952, where he currently lives. Inspired by the figural, fragmentary, and subjective qualities of Rodin's art, he began making sculpture in his late teens, and received his B.A. from the State University of New York at Binghamton in 1982. Gonzalez's early work consisted of small, hand-held sculptures and reliefs in cast plaster. By the early 1980s, he began welding steel armatures for larger scale sculptures of plaster and mixed media, which he increasingly manipulated through layering, burning, and sandblasting to achieve radically distorted forms and expressions. Gonzalez has consistently explored the figure as a central theme of his work, asserting that "only by making the body physically through materials and the process of sculpture can I express a sense of emotion and human presence needed to connect moments of coming into being with elements of decay and dissolution."

Gonzalez is highly inventive in his use of materials such as cast plaster, wax, carbon, tar, bones, cloth, and found objects combined with natural elements such as the flies, animal teeth, and feathers of *Scattered Remains.* His imagery has focused on the head, the body, and religious symbols such as the cross, with its association of personal torment. Extraordinarily prolific, he has created numerous individual pieces, group sculptures, indoor assemblages, and outdoor environments over the past fifteen years. Among Gonzalez's recent works is *Crosses,* which incorporated twenty-five thousand crosses appended to a group of five figures arranged in a concentrated circular space at the Everson Museum in Syracuse. In 1997, for the Neuberger Museum in Purchase, New York, he created *Tunnels,* an assembly of standing figures with conelike heads, fabricated of steel and cast plaster covered with asphalt and tar, merging into a landscape of mute openings. As with *Scattered Remains,* these installations reveal his fascination with repetition, variation, placement and scale, and his desire to achieve "tran-

sitional emotional states, where the bodies become enmeshed either with the groundscape, or with the objects attached to them." Citing both the contrasts and organic cycles simultaneously presented in *Scattered Remains,* the artist remarks: "I've always been incredibly attracted to contrasts. Creation and destruction are most deeply felt when they are integrated."—R.K.

1. *Magnolia Cemetery: The Proceedings at the Dedication of the Grounds* (Charleston, S.C.: Walker & James, 1851), 4.

Scattered Remains: Keeper

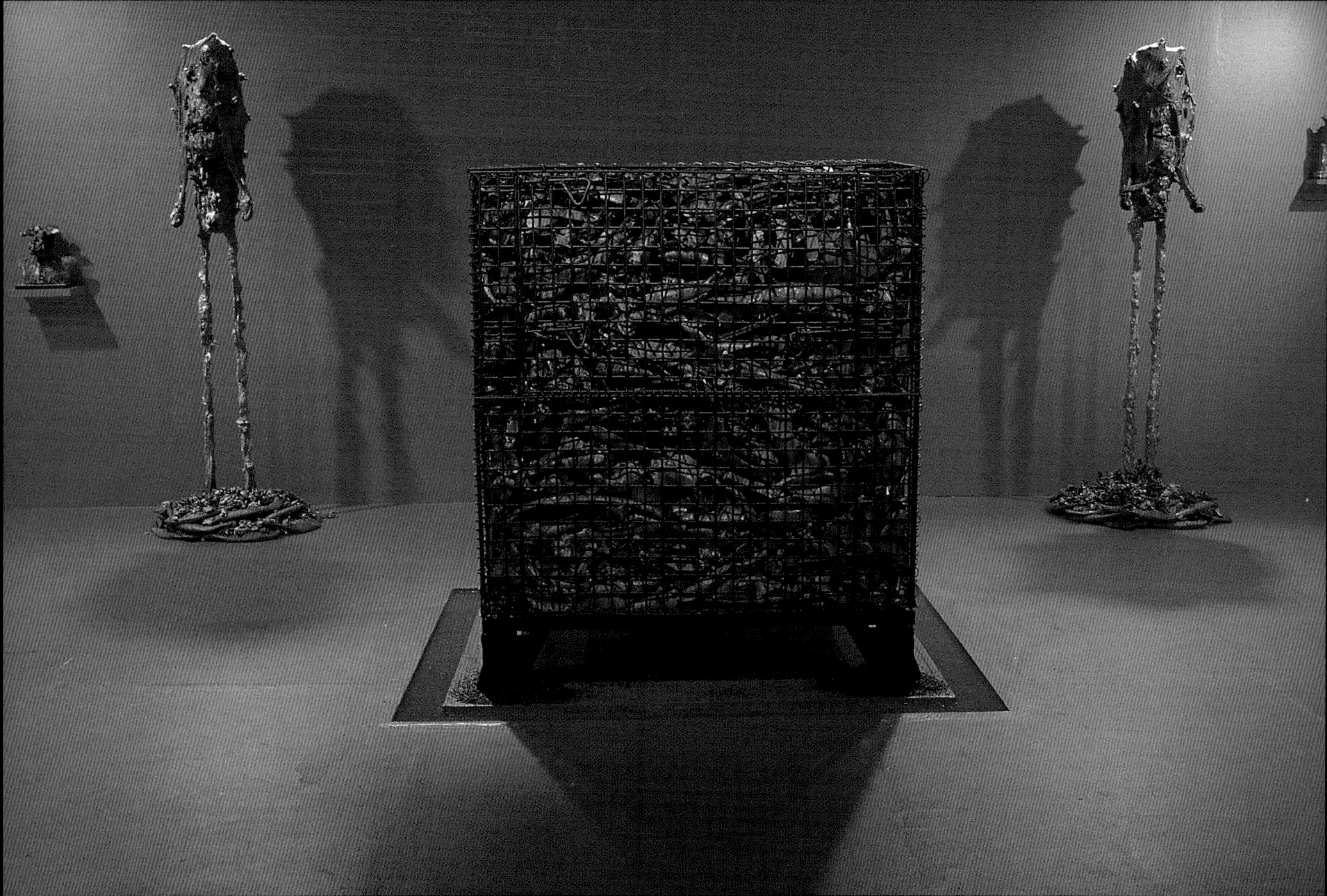

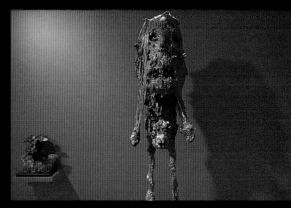

Martha Schwartz

Field Work

McLeod Plantation, James Island

Martha Schwartz has earned a reputation as one of the most original and provocative landscape designers at work in the United States today, transgressing some of the traditional boundaries between elite and popular culture, artificial and real versions of nature, and history and contemporary life. Trained as a visual artist and as a landscape architect, she straddles the two worlds, using the unorthodox materials and conceptual underpinnings of contemporary art to challenge some of the conventions of her design profession. She is widely known for temporary installations using ephemeral items such as bagels and Necco wafers. She toys with the stuff of vernacular culture, putting trees in tractor-tire planters and setting out rows of mass-produced, gilded concrete frogs. She frequently uses garish colors, which she sometimes paints directly onto the ground, and she has made gardens entirely out of artificial plants.

For the roof of the Whitehead Institute for Biomedical Research in Cambridge, Massachusetts, a space that could not bear the weight of soil and real plants, she employed Astroturf, plastic shrubs, and green paint to represent the idea of a garden. Dividing the space diagonally, she collaged together the raked gravel of a Japanese temple compound and the clipped formality of a classic French landscape. Calling the project *Splice Garden*, she created the piece as a commentary on both artificial life and the genetic research conducted in the building.

Despite her daring, Schwartz's recent commissions include both government and corporate projects. She created a new look for the plaza in front of the Jacob Javits Federal Office Building in Manhattan, where park benches laid out back-to-back in great looping shapes—suggestive of baroque parterres—curl around large turf mounds. She has also redesigned the plaza at Marcel Breuer's Department of Housing and Urban Development in Washington, D.C.

Schwartz's project for "Human/Nature" was located on an antebellum plantation

across the Ashley River from Charleston. It was composed of plain white cotton fabric panels hung from cables laid out in parallel lines. These ran from a row of 1855 slave cabins across an allée of live oak trees to a field of sweetgrass presently under cultivation for the city's African-American basketmakers. The cables were held up by steel posts; they were installed to form a continuous horizontal plane above the surface of the sloping ground. Consequently, the fabric panels were a mere 4 feet high near the slave cabins but lengthened to about 15 out in the field. They interrupted the dominant axis on the site, which leads up the double row of trees to the plantation house. They also connected the slave dwellings to the meadow, enforcing the relationship between domestic labor and field work in the lives of the cabins' former inhabitants.

Field Work employed a few familiar Schwartz strategies. She incorporated commonplace, mass-produced materials; she placed plots of white-painted lawn in front of each cabin, as if the structures were casting shadows toward the sweetgrass. She adapted the strategies of other contemporary artists to the interpretation of landscape: This work referenced Christo, both his draped fabric and his interest in exploring the social history of a place. Schwartz also made use of found elements on the site: The white panels played off black fabric already in use in the field to control weeds around the sweetgrass.

But *Field Work* was a sober, sometimes melancholy project from an often flamboyant and whimsical artist. It took on distinct attributes in different weather conditions and at various times of day. On a still morning, the cloth resembled sheets hung out to dry. Tethered at one corner, the panels evoked a fleet of sailboats on a windy day. In the mist, they sug-

gested row upon row of canvas tents, like some abandoned Civil War encampment.

If superficially distinct from her previous projects, *Field Work* manifested deeper analogies with them. Foremost was the concern it demonstrated for the workings of vernacular culture. The sheets, held up by countless wooden clothespins, alluded both to women's work and to domestic labor; it was Schwartz's intent to affirm the value of both. The selection of a cotton material was a deliberate reference to the importance of this plant in the economy of the antebellum South. Schwartz was also deeply concerned about the history of this particular landscape, especially the way its legible form represented the social relationships among plantation residents. She meant to subvert the dominant axis on the site; she wanted to enforce the relationship between the cabins and the field. But the fabric panels and grass paint together had the additional effect of creating a yard or private space around each house. Schwartz was figuratively giving the inhabitants independence from one another and from the plantation structure.

Field Work elicited controversy among the residents of James Island. Many called to complain when sections of it blew down in heavy winds. Some called it "Martha's Wash"; a writer to Charleston's newspaper, the *Post and Courier*, ridiculed the idea that clotheslines could be art; another complained that "what appears to be laundry" was a "disgrace, an insult to the late Willie McLeod and should be removed immediately." But an equal number wrote to endorse the project. One felt the work conjured up the spirits of the plantation's past inhabitants, the sheets suggesting "sails of long-gone vessels that . . . brought the Africans to Charleston as slaves."

Overall, the writer described Schwartz's effort as "a moving tribute to the persistent courage of generations of black slave women who humbly worked, gave birth, and died in the cabins of McLeod and elsewhere in our beloved South. Like all good art, it points no fingers; it conveys its subtle messages with visual symbols to those of us who try to see."[1]

Field Work may have been fragile and ephemeral, but it signaled an ambition for a tough and durable new form of cultural criticism. The interpretation of any site tends to privilege a master narrative; history is often told from the point of view of the rich and powerful. Schwartz said her intent was to "make it possible to see this landscape again" from a different perspective. She hoped people would recognize the combination of "horror and enchantment" she saw in the graceful allée of oaks sheltering the slave street. She wanted to bring out the ironies of the site: It is human nature to improve a landscape, she noted, but also to make captives of other people. By exhuming some of the African-American history of McLeod Plantation, she was able to suggest the multiple and contradictory narratives disguised in the landscapes of the low country. She gave voice temporarily to those whose stories are seldom told. —J.B.

1. The letters to the editor about Martha Schwartz's *Field Work* can be found in the *Post and Courier* for June 1, June 19, June 26, and July 15, 1997.

Adriaan Geuze

Cypress Swamp Garden

Cypress Gardens,
Moncks Corner

Although still in his thirties, Adriaan Geuze has built a significant practice as a landscape architect in his native Holland and across Europe. Born in Dordrecht in 1960 and trained at Wageningen Agricultural University, he established West 8 Landscape Architects in Rotterdam in 1987. The firm's recent projects have included the redesign of the landscape at Amsterdam's Schiphol Airport, plans for a residential development and park at the site of the former Riem airfield in Munich, and two public spaces for Rotterdam. One is a new square for the main city market; the other is the redesign of the Schouwburgplein (theater square) in the heart of the city by the Central Station, the municipal theater and concert hall. In recognition of his achievements, Geuze was the first landscape architect to receive the prestigious Rotterdam-Maaskant Prize for Young Architects, a distinction awarded in 1995.

Among the reasons Geuze was selected for this prize was his impact on the other de-sign professions. In addition to the customary parks and gardens, Geuze has created both individual objects and vast urban plans. He designed hundred-foot-tall coin-operated light towers that can be manipulated by pedestrians at the Schouwburgplein; he explored new housing typologies for the eight hundred thousand dwellings that Holland is expected to need by the year 2005 to shelter its swelling population. Geuze's versatility is a function of his view that landscape is not simply the counterpoint to the city, but the whole urban-rural constellation. As Geuze puts it, "The new city is a well-aired metropolis of villages, urban centers, suburbs, industrial areas, docks, airfields, woods, lakes, beaches, reserves, and the mono-cultures of hi-tech farming."[1]

Population density in the Netherlands, which approaches that of Japan, makes such macro-scale thinking almost unavoidable in that country. Designers have been creating new cities and towns in the polder (land created by diking and pumping out the sea) since

the end of World War II. Approximately seventy percent of the country's built environment has been created since 1945; much of its contemporary development is occurring in marginal lands, at the edges of traditional cities, or in abandoned industrial zones. Virtually every piece of land in the country is in use; open space exists not by default but because of rigorous planning.

Holland's dense population and relentless urbanization perhaps explain Geuze's attraction to the solitude of low-country cypress swamps. He was intrigued by Charleston, but seduced by the silent, unpeopled freshwater wetlands of Magnolia Plantation, Middleton Place, and Cypress Gardens. These are both wild and historical places. They are dominated by mature stands of cypress and tupelo and home to alligators, snakes, and fabulous birds. (The swamp garden at Magnolia Plantation was named for John James Audubon, as he collected some of the specimens there for his celebrated 1827-38 book *The Birds of America*.)

But they are also cultural artifacts. The wetlands at Magnolia and Cypress Gardens were created by slave labor in the eighteenth century as freshwater impoundments for inland rice cultivation. What looks "natural" in these instances are in fact constructed environments.

The same interplay of built and native elements characterized Geuze's creation at Cypress Gardens. The work was distinctly man-made, but it was conceived with the intention of intensifying a visitor's experience of the natural constituents of the swamp environment. It consisted of a simple rectangular pavilion, 30 by 60 feet and 20 feet high, built of slender steel posts connected by parallel strands of wire. These were draped with Spanish moss, an epiphyte of the bromeliad family native to the Southeast. Drawing both its moisture and its nutrients from the air, the moss stayed alive on the structure, changing color from an ashen gray when it was dry to gray-green when damp. The moss was hung in such a way that it formed a semitransparent veil when the walls were ob-

served head-on. Looking down the length of the sides, it appeared to be opaque.

Approached by a boardwalk that reached 50 feet out into the water, the pavilion contained two wooden decks at right angles to each other, on one of which was a pair of simple log benches made from the split halves of a toppled cypress found in the swamp. The structure enclosed a section of wetlands, framing several trees, but it was otherwise open to the sky and the water. Looking from the outside like a rectangle of moss suspended in the air, it was imagined by the artist as contemplative space in emulation of enclosed Japanese temple gardens such as the dry-stone composition at Roan-ji in Kyoto. As Geuze's associate Cyrus Clark told a reporter during construction, "The idea is to come inside the pavilion, sit at the edge and meditate. It's modeled after a Zen garden but without the religious inferences."[2]

The simplicity of this structure mandated close attention to its details in design. The

boardwalk that led out to the piece angled around a tree and changed levels, both to diminish its apparent length and to provide varying perspectives on the structure from the approach. The viewing platforms within the pavilion were given a serrated edge to add visual interest; they, too, were on different levels. To enhance the psychological experience of proximity to the water and its wildlife, neither walk nor platform had railings of any kind.

Geuze's design was motivated by a conviction that the experience of a landscape is intensified by the expansion and contraction of vistas. From a distance, the pavilion drew a visitor's eye; it became an object of curiosity and then a destination in the depth of the swamp. From the inside, the sense of enclosure focused attention on the basic elements of the swamp landscape: black water, aquatic plants, cypress trees, and Spanish moss. Out in the water within the pavilion was a sunning ramp to entice wildlife, including turtles and alligators. (The latter, being extremely shy, weren't seen venturing into the pavilion, though one could commonly be observed keeping an eye on the human activities from about 25 yards away.) From the viewing platform, the visitor looked back through the entrance and along a deck out over the open water. These openings provided a visual release from the compression of the interior, allowing one to extrapolate from this segment of the swamp an experience of the whole.

Geuze's project for "Human/Nature" was the most distant from Charleston—Cypress Gardens is about 25 miles up the Cooper River in neighboring Berkeley County. Once part of Dean Hall Plantation, one of the low country's largest rice plantations, the 170-acre swamp was planted with azaleas, camellias, dogwoods, and magnolias in the 1920s by busi-

nessman Benjamin Kittredge. Donated by his son to the city of Charleston in 1963, the site was given to Berkeley County in 1996 to become its first public park. The area near the visitor center is being developed with a freshwater aquarium, a butterfly house, and other educational facilities. The larger landscape is undergoing transformation by both human and natural agency. It is bracketed on two sides by industrial development, and its upland areas were shorn of a canopy of mature loblolly pines in Hurricane Hugo and are now growing up in maples and other hardwoods.

The swamp at Cypress Gardens is divided into three adjacent areas, each circled by a pathway. The section closest to the visitor center features cypress trees in deep, open water. The water is shallower in the middle segment and has more aquatic vegetation; the part farthest away is the wildest and most overgrown. Geuze's pavilion was in the middle section, and it took some effort to get there. It could be reached on foot or by flat-bottomed boat, but either way, it took about fifteen minutes. In both cases, the approach was part of the experience. Your pace slowed, preparing you for the solitude and serenity of the space. —J.B.

Project credits:
Design assistance: Trevor Bullen, Cyrus Clark, and Marnex Vink. Project constructed by Landscape Pavers, Ltd., Charleston.

1. Adriaan Geuze, quoted in *Adriaan Geuze/West 8: Landscape Architecture* (Rotterdam: 010 Publishers/Rotterdam-Maaskant Foundation, 1995), 8.

2. Cyrus Clark, quoted in Warren Wise, "Moss over Black Swamp is Part of Spoleto," *Post and Courier*, May 24, 1997, 4B.

Magdalena Abakanowicz
Crowd 1, 1986-1987
50 standing figures, burlap and resin

Magdalena Abakanowicz was born into an aristocratic family in Falenty, Poland, in 1930. As a child, she endured the Nazi invasion of Poland and the subsequent Communist takeover, which endowed her art with both a spirit of independence and of tragedy. She studied at the Academy of Fine Arts in Warsaw from 1950-54; beginning in the 1960s, she made monumental hanging sculptures out of woven fibers. She first came to international attention when her weavings won the gold medal at the São Paulo Biennial in 1965; in the 1970s, she began creating haunting groups of resin-stiffened burlap figures, which were often without arms or heads; in the 1980s, she expanded her range of materials to encompass bronze, stone, and wood. She is one of the world's most-renowned living sculptors, whose work has been featured in countless solo exhibitions and public installations. Her figures were the focus of a solo exhibition in the Polish pavilion at the Venice Biennale in 1980, and in 1982, she had solo exhibitions both at the Musée d'Art Moderne de la Ville de Paris and at the Museum of Contemporary Art in Chicago. These were followed by many other exhibitions around the globe. Among her commissions for large-scale sculptural installations are *Negev*, seven massive limestone disks for the Israel Museum in Jerusalem (1987); *Space of the Dragon*, ten monumental forms suggestive of animal heads for the Olympic Park in Seoul, South Korea (1988); and *Becalmed Beings*, a group of forty bronze seated figures seen from the back for Hiroshima, Japan (1992). Abakanowicz lives in Warsaw.

Selected references:
"Alterations"/Abakanowicz, exhibition catalog. Paris: Musée d'art moderne de la ville de Paris, 1982.
Brenson, Michael. "Survivor Art." *New York Times Magazine* (November 29, 1992): 47-54.
Magdalena Abakanowicz, exhibition catalog. Chicago: Museum of Contemporary Art and New York: Abbeville Press, 1982. Texts by Mary Jane Jacob, Jasia Reichardt, and Magdalena Abakanowicz.
Magdalena Abakanowicz: Memory, Silence, Life, exhibition catalog. Tokyo: Asahi Shimbun, 1991. Texts by Magdalena Abakanowicz, Mariusz Hermansdorfer, and Yoshiaki Inui.
Magdalena Abakanowicz: Recent Sculpture, exhibition catalog. Providence: Museum of Art, Rhode Island School of Design, 1993.
Magdalena Abakanowicz: War Games, exhibition catalog. New York: Institute for Contemporary Art, P.S.1 Museum, 1992. Texts by Michael Brenson, Alanna Heiss, and Magdalena Abakanowicz.
Rose, Barbara. *Magdalena Abakanowicz*. New York: Harry N. Abrams, 1994.

Thornton Dial was born in Emelle, Alabama, in 1928 and moved to Bessemer, near Birmingham, at age 13. His formal schooling ended after the fourth grade; thereafter, he worked at a variety of jobs, principally in the Pullman Standard boxcar factory. While at Pullman Standard, he also jobbed out as a highway worker, carpenter, bricklayer, house painter, pipefitter, and farmer. When the factory began laying off workers in the early 1980s, Dial set up a workshop in his backyard, where he and his sons made wrought-iron lawn and patio furniture, which in time assumed the quality of sculpture. By the late 1980s, Dial was devoting himself full-time to making art and had added painting and drawing to his repertoire. In 1993, he was given concurrent solo exhibitions at the New Museum of Contemporary Art and the Museum of American Folk Art, both in New York. His work was also featured prominently in two exhibitions organized to coincide with the 1996 Olympic games in Atlanta: a solo exhibition at the Carlos Museum of Emory University, and "Souls Grown Deep," the acclaimed exhibition of African-American vernacular art of the South.

Selected references:

Borum, Jenifer P. "Strategy of the Tiger: the World of Thornton Dial." *Folk Art* 18 (Winter 1993-94): 34-40.

McEvilley, Thomas. "The Missing Tradition." *Art in America* 85 (May 1997): 78-85, 137.

Smith, Dinitia. "Bits, Pieces and a Drive to Turn Them Into Art." *New York Times* (February 5, 1997): C9, 13.

Thornton Dial: Image of the Tiger, exhibition catalog. New York: Harry N. Abrams, 1993. Essays by Amiri Baraka and Thomas McEvilley.

Patrick Dougherty was born in Oklahoma in 1945 and raised in North Carolina. He earned a B.A. in English from the University of North Carolina and an M.A. in hospital administration from the University of Iowa. He enjoyed a successful career as an administrator but returned to Chapel Hill in 1975 to work as a carpenter and stone mason, while studying sculpture and art history. Inspired by building his own home in 1979, which a friend described as a work of art, he began to devote himself fully to sculpture, making work that evolved quickly from single pieces to large-scale environments. His sweeping, cyclonelike sculptures, woven of natural saplings, range from architectural forms and monumental sculptures to extended, multi-part environments. Dougherty's work has transformed over one hundred sites in North America, Europe, and Asia, including the Yorkshire Sculpture Park in England, the Laumeier Sculpture Park in St. Louis, the Smith College Museum of Art, and the American Craft Museum in New York City. He received one of the Awards in the Visual Arts from the Southeastern Center for Contemporary Art (1988), and has earned grants from the National Endowment for the Arts (1990), the Henry Moore Foundation (1993), and the Pollock-Krasner Foundation (1994).

Selected references:

Bloemink, Barbara. "Patrick Dougherty: Nesting Instincts." *Fiberarts* 18 (September/October 1991): 40-45.

Johnson, Linda L. *A Dialogue with Nature: Nine Contemporary Sculptors*, exhibition catalog. Washington, D.C.: Phillips Collection, 1992.

Patrick Dougherty: Crossing Over/An Installation, exhibition catalog. New York: American Craft Museum, 1996.

Patrick Dougherty: Site-Specific Installation, exhibition catalog. Kansas City, Mo.: Kemper Museum of Contemporary Art and Design, 1995.

Perfect Unity: Sculptors and Living Forms, exhibition catalog. St. Louis: Laumeier Sculpture Park, 1996.

Perreault, John. "Not Just for the Birds." *Review* (New York, October 1, 1996): 11-13.

Thornton Dial
***Respect for the Chair*, 1995**
mixed media

Patrick Dougherty
Intricate Loops, 1992
bamboo

Pearl Fryar
Topiary Garden, begun 1984
Bishopville, South Carolina

PHOTO: JERVEN MUSCH

Adriaan Geuze
Schouwburgplein by night
Rotterdam

Pearl Fryar is a self-taught topiary artist who was born in North Carolina in 1939. He lives in Bishopville, South Carolina, where he makes his living as a serviceman at the American National Can factory. After building a home in Bishopville, Fryar decided to create a garden in the hope of winning the "Yard of the Month" contest, which he did. The result is a fantastic, 3-acre topiary garden that attracts visitors from around the world, with hundreds of shrubs and trees cut and trained into hearts, fish bones, loops, circles, and mushrooms, with a 250-yard border of abstract, undulating shapes. Fryar has created topiaries for exhibition and for public and private gardens, including the South Carolina State Museum in Columbia and the Charlotte Botanical Garden.

Selected references:
Glasener, Erica. "Shear Inspiration: A Self-
    taught Artist Redefines Topiary." *Garden
    Design* (August/September 1996): 45-47.
Woodham, Tom. "The Cutting Hedge."
    Veranda vol. 10 (Fall 1996): 76-78.

Adriaan Geuze was born in Dordrecht, the Netherlands, in 1960 and educated at Wageningen Agricultural University, where he earned a master's degree in landscape architecture in 1987. The same year, he established his firm, West 8 Landscape Architects, in Rotterdam, where he continues to live and work. Among his recent projects are the redesign of the landscape for Amsterdam's Schiphol Airport; the new Schouwburgplein (theater square) and Market Square in Rotterdam; and plans for public parks in Berlin and Munich. The recipient of the Prix de Rome in 1990, he was awarded the prestigious Rotterdam-Maaskant

Award for Young Architects in 1995, the first landscape designer to be so honored. In addition to his practice, Geuze has taught at many design schools in Europe and the United States, including the Academie voor Bouwkunst, Amsterdam; the Academie voor Bouwkunst, Rotterdam; the Ecole Nationale Supérieure de Paysage de Versailles; and the Graduate School of Design at Harvard. Widely exhibited in Europe, his work was shown at the Storefront Gallery in New York in 1996.

Selected references:
Adriaan Geuze/West 8: Landscape Architecture.
    Rotterdam: 010 Publishers for the Rotterdam-
    Maaskant Foundation, 1995
Geuze, Adriaan, and West 8. *In Holland staat een
    huis.* Rotterdam: Netherlands Architecture
    Institute, 1995.
Lootsma, Bart. "Disconnecting Nature,
    Connecting Nature: West 8 in New York."
    Daidalos no. 65 (1997):104-109.
Vandermarliere, K., ed. *Het Landschap: Vier
    Internationale Landschapsontwerpers / The
    Landscape: Four International Landscape
    Designers.* Antwerp: de Singel, 1995.
Van Dijk, Hans. "Colonizing the Void." *A + U*
    no. 313 (October 1996): 76-79.
Weilacher, Udo. *Between Landscape Architecture
    and Land Art.* Basel and Boston: Birkhauser
    Verlag, 1996.

Ronald Gonzalez was born in Binghamton, New York, in 1952 and received his B.A. from the State University of New York at Binghamton, where he continues to live. His sculpture and sculptural installations feature large groups of humanlike figures made from a range of materials including welded steel, plaster, wax, tar, carbon, bones, insects, cloth, and found objects. He is represented in many public collections, including the Wadsworth Athenaeum in Hartford, Connecticut; the Everson Museum of Art in Syracuse; the Johnson Museum of Art at Cornell University; Florida International University of Art, Miami; and the Munson-Williams-Proctor Institute Museum of Art in Utica, New York. Gonzalez has received fellowships from the New York State Foundation for the Arts and the New York State Council on the Arts, and a grant from the Pollock-Krasner Foundation (1986). He has served residencies at Cornell University and the University of North Carolina at Chapel Hill.

Selected references:

Horned Figures, exhibition catalog. Scranton, Pennsylvania: Everhart Museum, 1995.

Pau-Llosa, Ricardo. "The Loyal Dog of Dread: The Art of Ronald Gonzalez." *Art Papers* 20 (May-June 1996): 65.

Ronald Gonzalez: Turning Bodies into Souls, exhibition catalog. New York: Intar Gallery, 1990. Essay by Ricardo Pau-Llosa.

Sadinsky, Rachel. *A Question of Faith: The Sculpture of Ronald Gonzalez*, exhibition catalog. Canton, New York: Richard F. Brush Art Gallery, St. Lawrence University, 1987.

Martha Jackson-Jarvis was born in Lynchburg, Virginia, in 1952 and moved to Philadelphia as a young teenager. She studied ceramics at Howard University in Washington, D.C., before earning a B.F.A. in sculpture and ceramics from Temple University in Philadelphia in 1975 and an M.F.A. in the same fields from Antioch University, Columbia, Maryland, in 1981. She maintains a studio near Washington, D.C., and has been active as a teacher at the Corcoran Gallery of Art in Washington, D.C., and the Maryland Institute College of Art, in Baltimore. She received a fellowship in sculpture from the National Endowment for the Arts (1986); an Arts International grant from the Lila Wallace-Reader's Digest Foundation to study mosaic techniques in Italy (1992); and a study grant from the Pilchuck Glass School, Seattle (1994). In 1996, the Washington Project for the Arts organized a solo exhibition of her work that was shown at the Corcoran Gallery of Art and at Maryland Art Place; in Baltimore. Among her recent projects is a mosaic and ceramic sculpture for the three-story atrium of the Prince George's County Courthouse in Upper Marlboro, Maryland.

Selected references:

The Decade Show: Frameworks of Identity in the 1980s, exhibition catalog. New York: Museum of Contemporary Hispanic Art, the New Museum of Contemporary Art, and the Studio Museum in Harlem, 1990.

Driskell, David C. *Contemporary Visual Expressions: The Art of Sam Gilliam, Martha Jackson-Jarvis, Keith Morrison, and William T. Williams*. Washington, D.C.: Smithsonian Institution Press, 1987.

Lippard, Lucy R. *Mixed Blessings. New Art in a Multicultural America*. New York: Pantheon Books, 1990.

Structuring Energy: Martha Jackson-Jarvis, 20 Years, exhibition catalog. Washington, D.C.: Washington Project for the Arts, 1996. Essays by John Beardsley and Nancy Grove.

Ronald Gonzalez
Crosses, 1996
plaster, wax, wire over welded steel

Martha Jackson-Jarvis
Table of Plenty, 1993-1994
clay, glass, copper, cement, wood

Len Jenshel

Best Western Mammoth, 1990

Hot Springs, Gardiner, Montana

Mary Lucier

Noah's Raven, 1993

mixed-media installation

Len Jenshel has been in the forefront of those photographers examining the changing American landscape. His monographs include *Hot Spots: America's Volcanic Landscape,* which pairs color images by Jenshel with black-and-white photographs by his wife, Diane Cook. Winner of the Golden Light/Ernst Haas Award for the best landscape photography book of 1996, the publication documents the indelible mark that volcanoes leave on the earth and in the imagination. Other books include *Travels in the American West* (1992), a stark and humorous look at the "wild frontier" that juxtaposes the romance of wilderness against the impact of tourism and development; and *Charmed Places* (1988), about the homes, gardens, and landscaping of nineteenth-century Hudson River painters. His photographs have been shown around the world, including solo exhibitions at the Yokohama Museum in Japan (1993); the Art Institute of Chicago (1984); and the International Center of Photography, New York (1983). Notable group exhibitions featuring his work include "Crossing the Frontier: the Developing West" at the San Francisco Museum of Modern Art (1996); and "Between Home and Heaven" at the National Museum of American Art, Smithsonian Institution, Washington, D.C. (1992). Jenshel's photography has appeared in *Aperture, House and Garden, New York Times Magazine, Life,* and *Harper's,* among numerous other publications.

Selected references:

Byrne, David. *True Stories.* New York: Viking Penguin, 1986.

Charmed Places: Hudson River School Artists and Their Homes. New York: Harry N. Abrams, 1988.

Cook, Diane, and Len Jenshel. *Hot Spots: America's Volcanic Landscape.* Boston: Bulfinch Press, Little Brown & Company, 1996.

Euaclaire, Sally. *The New Color Photography.* New York: Abbeville Press, 1981.

Forresta, Merry A. *Between Home and Heaven,* exhibition catalog. Washington, D.C.: Smithsonian Institution Press, 1992.

Phillips, Sandra. *Crossing the Frontier: Photographs of the Developing West,* exhibition catalog. San Francisco: San Francisco Museum of Modern Art, 1996.

Travels in the American West. Washington, D.C.: Smithsonian Institution Press, 1992.

Mary Lucier was born in Bucyrus, Ohio, in 1944. She graduated from Brandeis University in 1965 and now lives and works in New York City. Known as a pioneer in the field of video art, she has produced more than thirty-five mixed media installations since 1973. Her projects are among the first video installations to have been acquired by major museums, including the Whitney Museum of American Art, New York, and the San Francisco Museum of Modern Art. Recent solo exhibitions have introduced ambitious new works, including *Noah's Raven,* a four-channel laserdisc installation for eight monitors in an arrangement of trees and forklifts with a hanging fossil, commissioned by the Toledo Museum of Art in 1993; *Oblique House (Valdez),* an interactive mixed-media installation in a specially constructed house, which premiered the same year at Montage '93 in Rochester, New York; and *Last Rites (Positano),* based on an episode in family history and incorporating projection, sound, photographs, and domestic furniture, first shown at the Lennon, Weinberg Gallery in New York, in 1995. She is the recipient of numerous grants and awards, including those from the John Simon

Guggenheim Memorial Foundation, the American Film Institute, the Jerome Foundation, the National Endowment for the Arts, the New York State Council on the Arts, and the Anonymous was a Woman Foundation. Her work is the subject of a forthcoming book from *Performing Arts Journal* in conjunction with Johns Hopkins University Press, Baltimore.

Selected references:

Barlow, Melinda. "The Architecture of Image and Sound: Dwelling in the Work of Mary Lucier." *Art Journal* 54 (Winter 1995): 53-57.

_____. "Personal History, Cultural Memory: Mary Lucier's Ruminations on Body and Land." *Afterimage* 21 (November 1993): 8-12.

Hagan, Charles. "The Unsolved Mysteries of Memory." *The New York Times* (April 7, 1995), Weekend Section.

Heartney, Eleanor. *Noah's Raven: A Video Installation by Mary Lucier*, exhibition catalog. Toledo, Ohio: Toledo Musem of Art, 1993.

Lucier, Mary. "Light and Death," in *Illuminating Video: An Essential Guide to Video Art*, 457-63. New York: Aperture Books, 1991.

"Mary Lucier" (interview with Peter Doroshenko). *Journal of Contemporary Art* 3 (Fall/Winter 1990): 81-89.

Russell, John. "Mary Lucier." *New York Times* (November 10, 1989).

Esther Mahlangu was born in Middleburg, Transvaal, South Africa, in 1936 and learned Ndebele art from her mother and grandmother. As the most widely known practitioner of Ndebele painting, she has traveled internationally to execute commissions in Johannesburg, the United States, France, Switzerland, Portugal, and Japan. In her home village of Kwandebele, Mahlangu runs a

school to teach young people in her community to paint and create beadwork. She has also served as a resident artist at the Botshabelo Museum, an open-air institution designed to showcase Ndebele arts. In 1989, Mahlangu painted a replica of her house at the Centre Georges Pompidou in Paris as part of the international exhibition "Magiciens de la Terre." In 1991, she became the first female artist commissioned to paint a BMW "art car," which was exhibited at Documenta 9 in Kassel, Germany (1992). In addition to her work for the Spoleto Festival, her recent tours to the United States have included a mural created in conjunction with an exhibition at the National Museum of Women in the Arts, Washington, D.C. (1994).

Selected references:

Angelou, Maya, and Margaret Courtney-Clark. *My Painted House, My Friendly Chicken, and Me.* New York: Clarkson Potter, 1994. A children's book with photographs of Ndebele art, including work by Esther Mahlangu.

Goldblatt, David. *Ndebele: The Art of an African Tribe.* New York: Rizzoli, 1986.

Magiciens de la Terre, exhibition catalog. Paris: Editions du Centre Pompidou, 1989.

Powell, Ivor. *Ndebele—A People and Their Art.* New York: Cross River Press, 1995.

Young, Lucie. "Currents: A Striking Archway, Out of Africa." *New York Times* (April 10, 1997).

Herb Parker was born in 1953 in Elizabeth City, North Carolina. He received his B.F.A. and M.F.A. degrees from East Carolina University in Greenville, North Carolina, and now teaches at the College of Charleston. Since 1983, Parker has been creating environmental

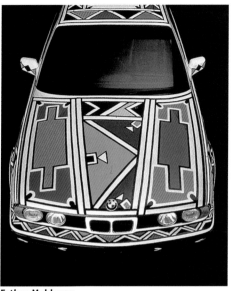

Esther Mahlangu
BMW Art Car, 1991

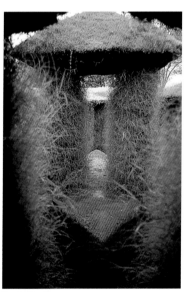

Herb Parker
Temple: Transit, 1994
sod, steel, rammed earth

163

structures—living architectural forms, such as caves, domes, or temples—using sod planted over steel structures. He has built these structures throughout the United States, Canada, and abroad, at the South Carolina Botanical Garden in Clemson, South Carolina; the Toronto Sculpture Garden; the Southeast Center for Contemporary Art in Winston-Salem, North Carolina; Art Park in Lewiston, New York; and Arte Sella in Trentino, Italy. Parker has received grants from the Southern Arts Federation/National Endowment for the Arts and the Ford Foundation.

Selected references:

Brennan, Anne G. *Herb Parker: Temple/Transit,* exhibition catalog. Wilmington, N.C.: St. John's Museum of Art, 1994.

Lafitte, Polly. *Sculpture South 94,* exhibition catalog. Columbia: South Carolina State Museum, 1994.

Szakacs, Dennis. "Sod Installation: Herb Parker's Closure Passage." *Document* 1, Southeastern Center for Contemporary Art, 3-5.

Martha Schwartz was born in Philadelphia in 1950 and was educated at the University of Michigan and the Harvard Graduate School of Design, where she has taught as an adjunct professor of landscape architecture since 1992. She established her firm, Martha Schwartz, Inc., in 1982 for the practice of landscape design, with a particular emphasis on projects for private clients and site-specific public art commissions; the firm presently has offices in Cambridge, Massachusetts, and San Francisco, California. She has worked in partnership with other landscape architects, notably Peter Walker and Ken Smith; and has collaborated with architects including Philip Johnson, Arquitectonica, and Arata Isozaki. Recent projects include the redesign of Federal Plaza at the Jacob K. Javits Federal Office Building in lower Manhattan; a plaza for the United States Courthouse in Minneapolis; and master planning for the 2000 Olympic Games in Sydney, Australia. The recipient of several design awards from the American Society of Landscape Architects, she has also been awarded public art commissions in Seattle, Miami, and Boston.

Selected references:

Cooper, Guy, and Gordon Taylor. *Paradise Transformed: The Private Garden for the Twenty-First Century.* New York: Monacelli Press, 1996.

Gillette, Jane Brown. "Self-Portrait." *Landscape Architecture* 87 (February 1997): 70-75, 88-92.

Landecker, Heidi, ed., and Elizabeth K. Meyer. *Martha Schwartz: Transfiguration of the Commonplace.* Washington, D.C.: Spacemaker Press, 1997.

Weilacher, Udo. *Between Landscape Architecture and Land Art.* Basel and Boston: Birkhauser Verlag, 1996.

Philip Simmons was born in 1912 on Daniel Island, South Carolina, and lives and works in Charleston. Since mid-century, Simmons has produced more than 250 examples of finely wrought ornamental gates, fences, and architectural elements throughout Charleston for private residences and public buildings such as the First Baptist and St. Michael's churches. In 1982, the National Endowment for the Arts awarded him its National Heritage Fellowship, and he was commissioned to execute an iron work on-site at the

PHOTO: ALAN WARD

Martha Schwartz
Federal Plaza, 1996
New York

Smithsonian's Festival of American Folklife on the Mall in Washington, D.C. The result was the Star and Fish Gate, now in the collection of the National Museum of American History. Simmons' work is also represented in the Museum of International Folk Art in Santa Fe, New Mexico, and in the South Carolina State Museum in Columbia.

Selected references:

Vlach, John Michael. *Charleston Blacksmith: The Work of Philip Simmons.* Athens: University of Georgia Press, 1981; revised ed. Columbia: University of South Carolina Press, 1992.

Vlach, John Michael. "Philip Simmons: Afro-American Blacksmith," in *Black People and Their Culture,* ed. Linn Shapiro. Washington: Smithsonian Institution Press, 1976.

Twiggs, Leo F. *Keeper of the Gate: Designs in Wrought Iron by Philip Simmons, Master Blacksmith,* exhibition catalog. Charleston: Philip Simmons Foundation, 1993.

Watson, Tom. "Hammering out a Vision." *Southern Accents* 20 (September/October 1997): 104-06.

Watson, Tom. "In Profile, Philip Simmons: A Wrought-iron Artist Hammers out a Legacy." *Art & Antiques* 17 (March 1994): 128.

Charles Simonds was born in 1945 in New York City and was educated at the University of California at Berkeley and at Rutgers University, from which he received an M.F.A. in 1969. In 1970, he enacted his "birth" as an artist, emerging naked from a clay pit in New Jersey. The same year, on window ledges and building edges on the streets of New York, he began constructing small, clay dwellings for an imaginary race of seminomadic "little people." Although he initially resisted invitations to install his dwellings in museums,

he presented a solo exhibition of his work at the Centre National d'Art Contemporain in Paris in 1975 and in 1976 took part in the "Projects" exhibition series at the Museum of Modern Art. Since then, he has exhibited his sculptures widely and has created site-specific environments for numerous institutions around the world. A major American retrospective of his work was organized by the Museum of Contemporary Art, Chicago, in 1981; the exhibition traveled to the Los Angeles County Museum and the Solomon R. Guggenheim Museum, New York, among others. A European retrospective was organized in 1994 and shown at the Centre Cultural de la Fundació "la Caixa" in Barcelona and the Galerie Nationale du Jeu de Paume in Paris. In recent years, his work has grown increasingly large and figural, with fantastical architecture combined with bodily and facial imagery. Simonds currently lives and works in New York.

Selected references:

Abadie, Daniel. *Charles Simonds* (Art/Cahier 2). Paris: SMI, 1975.

Beardsley, John. "Hybrid Dreams." *Art in America* 83 (March 1995): 92-97.

Charles Simonds, exhibition catalog. Barcelona: Centre Cultural de la Fundació "la Caixa" and Paris: Editions du Jeu de Paume, 1994.

Lippard, Lucy, and Charles Simonds. "Microcosm to Macrocosm/Fantasy World to Real World." *Artforum* 12 (February 1974): 36-39.

Neff, John H. *Charles Simonds,* exhibition catalog. Chicago: Museum of Contemporary Art, 1981.

PHOTO: WILLIAM STRUHS

Philip Simmons
Snake Gates
Christopher Gadsden House, Charleston

Charles Simonds
Head, 1993
clay and plaster

Spoleto Festival U.S.A. gratefully acknowledges the following individuals, institutions, and businesses for their generous assistance in organizing the "Human/Nature" exhibition:

Sarah Amos

William Arnett

Ashley Hall School
　Margaret C. McDonald
　Meyriel J. Edge

Bennett Hofford Company

Berkeley County
　Jim Rozier

Brooks Sign Company

Sandra Campbell

Carolina Nurseries, Inc.

Carolina Prints
　Johnson Hagood

City of Charleston
　Mayor Joseph P. Riley, Jr.
　Amanda Barton
　Danny Burbage
　Steve Livingston
　Danny Molony
　Ellen Moryl
　Tom O'Brien

Rossie Colter

Cypress Gardens
　Ken Alfieri
　Dwight Williams

Chapter Two Bookstore
　Susan Davis

Jeffrey Day

Mr. and Mrs. Herbert A. DeCosta, Jr.

Patricia DeHond

Ann deSaussure

Nicholas Drake

Gibbes Museum of Art
　Paul Figueroa
　India Hopper
　Greg Jenkins
　Shellie Williams

Historic Charleston Foundation
　Carter L. Hudgins
　Tom Savage
　Carol Borchert
　Robert Leath
　Renée Marshall
　Jason Neville

Carmen Kovens

Rick Lambert, PE

Owen Riley Lee

Patricia Leighton

Robert Maerlender

Magnolia Cemetery Trust
　G. Simms McDowell III
　Ted Phillips
　Beverly Donald

Marlborough Gallery Inc.
　Phillip A. Bruno

Mr. and Mrs. Frank McCann

Mr. and Mrs. Joseph H. McGee

Betty Ann Mead

Medical University of South Carolina
　Layton McCurdy

Middleton Place
　Charles P. Duell
　Pat A. Kennedy

Jerry Poore

David L. Rawle

St. John's Reformed
　Episcopal Church
　Right Reverend James C. West, Sr.

St. Luke's Reformed
　Episcopal Church
　Reverend Dr. Julius Barnes

Brook Scott

Philip Simmons Foundation

Mark Sloan, Halsey Gallery

Matt Sloan, Daniel Island
　Development Corporation

South Carolina Arts Commission
　Harriet Green
　Marion Draine

South Carolina Coastal
　Conservation League

South Carolina Historical Society

Southern Shade Nurseries

Barbara Stender

Debbie Stocker

William Struhs

Linzy and Karen Washington

Sheila Wertimer, ASLA

Viola Ziambe

Mr. and Mrs. Stephen Ziff

166　**Acknowledgments**

Support for this exhibition was provided by

The John and Kathleen Rivers Foundation

The Rockefeller Foundation

Jane Smith Turner Foundation

Directors

Mr. Joe Anderson

Mrs. Ann Apple

Mr. Carswell Berlin

Mrs. Philip Blumenthal

Mrs. Andres Boulton

Mrs. William Branstrom

Mrs. Jackson Burnett

Mr. Homer C. Burrous

Mr. Wayland H. Cato, Jr.

Mrs. Joan Sasser Coker

Mr. Leonard Coleman

Mr. Herbert A. DeCosta, Jr.

Mrs. Ellen Dudash

Mr. Darrell C. Ferguson

Mrs. Kirkman Finlay, Jr.

Mr. Carl W. Flesher, Jr.

Mrs. Nancy M. Folger

Mr. Eric G. Friberg

Mr. Carl I. Gable

Mr. John B. Hagerty

Mr. William Hewitt

Mrs. Martha Rivers Ingram

Mrs. Harriet H. Keyserling

Mrs. John C. Land, III

Dr. Thomas Leland

Mr. Ernest Levenstein

Mrs. D. Elizabeth Marshall

Mr. David Maybank

Mr. John Mayberry

Dr. Thomas Godfrey

Quattlebaum

Mr. John Rainey

Mrs. Susan Ravenel

Mrs. Ann Y. Riley

Mrs. John M. Rivers, Jr.

Judge Alexander M. Sanders, Jr.

Mrs. Joan Sarnoff

Mr. A.J. Signorile

Mr. Lucas Simonds

Ms. Lea Hillman Simonds

Mrs. G. Dana Sinkler

Mrs. Charlotte Sloan

Mr. Joel A. Smith, III

Mr. W. Thomas Smith

Mr. Henry B. Smythe, Jr.

Mr. Melvin Solomon

Mr. Will Spence

Mr. Randolph Updyke

Mrs. Jack Vane

Mrs. William C. Westmoreland

Mr. Joe Whitmore

Chairman Emeritus

Mr. Homer C. Burrous

Chairman Emeritus

Mr. Ross Markwardt

Chairman Emeritus

Dr. Theodore Stern

Chairman Emeritus

Mr. Charles S. Way, Jr.

Human|Nature: Art and Landscape In Charleston And The Low Country

Curator

John Beardsley

Associate Curator

Roberta Kefalos

Festival Staff

General Director

Nigel Redden

Director of Operations

Nunally Kersh

Director of Development

Julia Forster

Director of Marketing and Public Relations

Marie Lawson

Director of Finance

Anastasia G. Gandy

Production Managers

John H. Paull, III

Rhys Williams

Human|Nature Crew

Project Installation Coordinator

T. Kevin Fisher

Project Installation Crew

Jeni Adams, Joe Avellino, Sara Bettinger, Steve Bright, Chris Burrel, Mike Carrico, Stacey Chalmers, David Costello, Diane Daubert, Joe Dickerson, Gregg Eddins, Bob Edwards, Sharon Gilchrist, Frank Hart, Beth Heerman, Rick Hill, Jerry Hoppe, Matt Kady, Tess L'Heureux, Andy Lindhal, John Alex Mason, Driscoll Otto, Tim Sullivan, Terry Tucker, Mike Voytko, Kate Yungblut

Administration

Assistant to General Director

Anja Urbanski

Assistant to Director of Operations

Dixie Townsend

Receptionist

Philip Gervais

Education Coordinator

Nina Custer*

Housing Coordinator

Brad Erickson*

Transportation Coordinator

Todd Bentjen*

Development

Director of Special Events

Lisa Weber

Development Systems Manager

Annette Sheppard

Development Associate for Grants

Jennifer Stimpson

Development Assistant

Jessica Melton

Marketing and Public Relations

Marketing and Public Relations Associate/Group Sales Manager

Ann-Marie Edwards

Public Relations Associate

Chester Jacinto*

Marketing & Public Relations Intern

Jessica Bluestein*

Merchandising Coordinator

Margaret Schwab*

Assistant Merchandising Coordinator

Jill Remmers*

Photographer

William Struhs*

Finance

General Accounting Manager

Todd Nimmich

Accounting/Payroll Clerk

Lorrie Passailaigue

* Indicates Seasonal Staff

Support for the printing of this book has been provided in part by the Elizabeth Firestone–Graham Foundation.

Patrick Dougherty

The Path of Least Resistance